Edward Earl of Clarendon

The History of the Rebellion and Civil Wars in England, begun in the Year 1641

Volume IV.

Edward Earl of Clarendon

The History of the Rebellion and Civil Wars in England, begun in the Year 1641
Volume IV.

ISBN/EAN: 9783742812667

Manufactured in Europe, USA, Canada, Australia, Japa

Cover: Foto ©ninafisch / pixelio.de

Manufactured and distributed by brebook publishing software (www.brebook.com)

Edward Earl of Clarendon

The History of the Rebellion and Civil Wars in England, begun in the Year 1641

THE

HISTORY

OF THE

REBELLION AND CIVIL WARS

IN

ENGLAND,

Begun in the Year 1641.

With the precedent Passages, and Actions, that contributed thereunto, and the happy End, and Conclusion thereof by the KING's blessed RESTORATION, and RETURN upon the 29th of *May*, in the Year 1660.

Written by the Right Honorable

EDWARD Earl of CLARENDON,

Late Lord High Chancellor of *England*, Privy-Counsellor in the Reigns of King CHARLES the First and the Second.

Κτῆμα ἐς ἀεί. *Thucyd.*
Ne quid Falsi dicere audeat, ne quid Veri non audeat. Cicero.

VOL IV.

BASIL:
Printed and sold by J. J. TOURNEISEN.
MDCCXCVIII.

THE
History of the Rebellion, etc.
BOOK V.

It was within very few days after, that the King, exceedingly displeased and provoked with the Keeper's behaviour, sent an Order to the Lord *Falkland*, " to require the Seal from him;" in which the King was very positive, though he was not resolved to what hand to commit it. His Majesty wished them (for he always included the other Two in such references) to consider, " whether he should give it " to the Lord Chief Justice *Banks* (against whom he made some objection himself) " or into the hands " of Mr. *Selden*; and to send their opinions to him." The Order was positive for requiring it from the present Officer, but they knew not who to advise for a Successor. The Lord Chief Justice *Banks* appeared to be as much afraid, as the other; and not thought equal to that Charge, in a time of so much disorder; though otherwise he was a Man of great abilities, and unblemished integrity; they did not doubt of Mr. *Selden*'s Affection to the King, but withal they knew him so well, that they concluded he would absolutely refuse the place, if it were offered to him. He was in years, and of a tender constitution; he had for many years enjoyed his ease, which he loved; was rich; and would not have made a Journey to *York*, or have lain out of his own bed, for any Preferment; which he had never affected.

Being all Three of one mind, that it would not be fit to offer it to the one or the other; hereupon Mr. *Hyde* told them the conference he had with the Keeper, and the professions he had made; and was very confident, that he would very punctually perform it; and therefore proposed, that " they might, " with their Opinions of the other Persons, like- " wise advise his Majesty to suspend his resolution " concerning the Lord Keeper, and rather to write " kindly to him, to bring the Seal to his Majesty, " instead of sending for the Seal itself, and cast him " off; " and offered to venture his own credit with the King, that the Keeper would comply with his Majesty's commands. Neither of them were of his opinion; and had both no esteem of the Keeper, nor believed, that he would go to his Majesty, if he were sent for, but that he would find some trick to excuse himself; and therefore were not willing, that Mr. *Hyde* should venture his Reputation upon it. He desired them then " to consider how absolutely " necessary it was, that the King should first resolve " into what hand to put the Seal, before he removed " it; for that it could not be unemployed one hour, " but that the whole Justice of the Kingdom would " be put out of order, and draw a greater and a " juster clamor, than had been yet: That there " was as much care to be taken, that it should not " be in the power of any man to refuse it, which " would be yet more prejudicial to his Majesty. He " desired them above all, to weigh well, that the " business consisted only in having the Great Seal in

"the place where his Majesty resolved to be; and if
"the Keeper would keep his promise, and desired
"to serve the King, it would be unquestionably the
"best way, that He and the Seal were both there:
"if, on the other side, he were not an honest Man,
"and cared not for offending the King, he would
"then refuse to deliver it; and inform the Lords of
"it: who would justify him for his disobedience, and
"reward and cherish him; and he must then here-
"after serve Their turn; the mischief whereof would
"be greater, than could be easily imagined: and his
"Majesty's own Great Seal should be every day
"used against him, nor would it be possible in many
"Months to procure a New one to be made.

These Objections appeared of weight to them; and they Resolved to give an account of the whole to the King, and to expect his Order: and both the Lord *Falkland*, and Mr. *Hyde*, writ to his Majesty, and sent their Letters away that very Night. The King was satisfied with the Reasons, and was very glad that Mr. *Hyde* was so confident of the Keeper; though, he said, " he remained still in doubt; and " Resolved that he would, such a day of the Week " following, send for the Keeper and the Seal;" and that it should be, as had been advised, upon a *Saturday* Afternoon, as soon as the House of Lords should rise; because then no notice could be taken of it till *Monday*. Mr. *Hyde*, who had continued to see the Keeper frequently, and was confirmed in his confidence of his Integrity, went now to him; and finding him firm to his Resolution and of opinion, in regard of the high Proceedings of the Houses, that it should not be long deferred; he told him, "that he might expect a Messenger the next Week, "and that he should once more see him, when he "would tell him the Day; and that he would then "go himself away before him to *York*;" with which he was much pleased, and it was agreed between the Three, that it was now time, that he should be gone (the King having sent for him some time before) after a day or two; in which time the Declaration of the nineteenth of *May* would be passed.

On the *Saturday* following, between two and three of the Clock in the Afternoon, Mr. *Elliot*, a Groom of the Bed-Chamber to the Prince, came to the Keeper, and found him alone in the Room where he used to sit, and delivered him a Letter from the King in his own hand; wherein he required him, with many expressions of kindness and esteem, "to "make haste to him;" and if his indisposition (for he was often troubled with gravel and sharpness of Urine) "would not suffer him to make such haste "upon the Journey, as the occasion required, that "he should deliver the Seal to the Person who gave "him the Letter; who, being a strong young Man, "would make such haste as was necessary; and that "he might make his own Journey, by those degrees "which his Health required." The Keeper was surprised with the Messenger, whom he did not like; and more when he found that he knew the contents of the Letter, which, he hoped, would not have been communicated to any Man, who should be sent: He Answered him with much reservation, and when the other with bluntness, as he was no polite Man, demanded the Seal of him, which he had not thought of putting out of his own hands; he Answered him, "that he would not deliver it into any hands, but "the King's;" but presently recollecting himself, and looking over his Letter again, he quickly considered, that it would be hazardous to carry the Seal himself such a Journey; and that if by any pursuit of him, which he could not but suspect, he should be seized upon, the King would be very unhappily disappointed of the Seal, which he had reason so much to depend upon; and that his misfortune would be wholly imputed to his own fault and infidelity (which without doubt he abhorred with his heart) and the only way to prevent that mischief, or to appear innocent under it, was to deliver the Seal to the Person trusted by the King himself to receive it; and so, without telling him any thing of his own purpose, he delivered the Seal into his hands; who forthwith put himself on his Horse, and with wonderful expedition presented the Great Seal into his Majesty's own hands; who was infinitely pleased with It, and with the Messenger.

The Keeper, that Evening, pretended to be indisposed, and that he would take his rest early, and therefore that no body should be admitted to speak with him: and then he called Serjeant *Lee* to him, who was the Serjeant who waited upon the Seal, and in whom he had great Confidence, as he well might; and told him freely, "That he was resolved the next "Morning, to go to the King, who had sent for him; "that he knew well, how much malice he should "contract by it from the Parliament, which would "use all the means they could to apprehend him; and he himself knew not how he should perform the Journey, therefore he put himself entirely into his hands; that he should cause his Horses to be ready against the next Morning, and only his own Groom to attend them, and he to guide the best way, and that he would not impart it to any other Person." The honest Serjeant was very glad of the Resolution, and cheerfully undertook all things for the Journey; and so sending the Horses out of the Town, the Keeper put himself in his Coach very early the next Morning, and as soon as they were out of the Town, He and the Serjeant, and one Groom, took their Horses, and made so great a Journey that day, it being about the beginning of *June*, that before the end of the third day, he kissed the King's hand at *York*.

He had purposely procured the House of Peers to be Adjourned to a later hour, in the Morning for *Monday*, than it used to be. *Sunday* passed without any Man's taking notice of the Keeper's being absent; and many, who knew that he was not at his House, thought he had been gone to *Cranford*, to his Country-House, whither he frequently went on *Saturday* nights, and was early enough at the Parliament on *Monday* mornings; and so the Lords the more willingly consented to the later Adjournements for those days. But on *Monday* Morning, when it was known when, and in what manner he had left his House, the confusion in both Houses was very great; and they who had thought that their interest was so great in him, that they knew all his thoughts, and had valued themselves, and were valued by others, upon that account, hung down their heads, and were even distracted with shame: However they could not but conclude that He was out of their reach before the Lords met; yet to show their indignation against him, and it may be in hope that his Infirmities would detain him long in the Journey (as no body indeed thought that he could have performed it, with that expedition) they issued out such a Warrant for the apprehending him, as had been in the case of the foulest Felon or Murderer; and Printed it, and caused it to be dispersed by Expresses, over all the Kingdom with great haste. All which circumstances both before, and after the Keeper's Journey to *York*, are the more particularly, and at large set down, out of justice to the memory of that noble Person; whose Honor suffered then much in the opinion of many, by the confident report of the Person, who was sent for, and received the Seal, and who was a loud and bold Talker, and desired to have it believed, that his Manhood had ravished the Great Seal from the Keeper, even in spite of his teeth; which, how impossible soever in itself, found too much Credit; and is therefore cleared by this very true and punctual Relation, which in truth is but due to him.

But the Trouble and Distraction, which at this time possessed them, was visibly very great; and their dejection such, that the same day the Earl of *Northumberland* (who had been of another temper) moved, " that a Committee might be appointed, to consider " how there might be an Accommodation between " the King and his People, for the Good, Happiness,

BOOK V.

"and Safety of both King and Kingdom;" which Committee was appointed accordingly.

This temper of Accommodation troubled them not long, new Warmth and Vigor being quickly infused into them by the unbroken, and undaunted Spirits of the House of Commons; which, to show how little they valued the Power or Authority of the King, though supported by having now his Great Seal by him, on the 26th of *May* agreed on a new Remonstrance to the People; in which, the Lords concurring, they informed them,

The two Houses Remonstrance May 26, 1642.

"That although the great Affairs of the Kingdom, and the miserable bleeding Condition of the Kingdom of *Ireland* afforded them little leisure, to spend their time in Declarations, and in Answers, and Replies, yet the Malignant Party about his Majesty taking all occasions to multiply Calumnies upon the Houses of Parliament, and to publish sharp invectives, under his Majesty's Name against them, and their proceedings (a new Engine they had invented to heighten the Distractions of this Kingdom, and to beget, and increase distrust, and disaffection between the King, and his Parliament, and the People) they could not be so much wanting to their own Innocency, or to the duty of their Trust, as not to clear themselves from those false aspersions, and (which was their chiefest care) to disabuse the People's minds, and open their Eyes, that, under the false shows, and pretexts of the Law of the Land, and of their own Rights, and Liberties, they may not be carried into the Road-way, that leadeth to the utter Ruin, and

"Subversion thereof. A late occasion that those
" wicked Spirits of division had taken to defame, and
" indeed to arraign the proceedings of both Houses of
" Parliament, had been from the Votes of the 28th of
" *April*, and their Declaration concerning the busi-
" ness of *Hull*, which because they put forth, before
" they could send their Answer concerning that
" matter unto his Majesty, those mischievous Instru-
" ments of dissension, between the King, and the
" Parliament, and the People, whose chief Labor,
" and Study, was to misrepresent their Actions to
" his Majesty, and to the Kingdom, would needs
" interpret this as an Appeal to the People, and a
" declining of all intercourse between his Majesty
" and them; as if they thought it to no purpose, to
" endeavour any more, to give his Majesty satis-
" faction; and, without expecting any longer their
" Answer, under the Name of a Message from his
" Majesty to both Houses, they themselves had in-
" deed made an Appeal to the People, as the Message
" itself did in a manner grant it to be, offering to join
" issue with them in that way, and in the nature there-
" of did clearly show itself to be no other; therefore
" They would likewise Address their Answer to the
" Kingdom, not by way of Appeal (as they were
" charged) but to prevent them from being their
" own Executioners, and from being persuaded
" under false colors of defending the Law, and their
" own Liberties, to destroy both with their own
" hands, by taking their Lives, Liberties, and Estates
" out of Their hands, whom they had chosen, and
" intrusted therewith, and resigning them up unto

"some evil Counsellors, about his Majesty, who could lay no other foundation of their own greatness, but upon the Ruin of this, and, in It, of all Parliaments; and in Them, of the true Religion, and the Freedom of this Nation. And these, they said, were the Men that would perfuade the People, that both Houses of Parliament, containing all the Peers, and reprefenting all the Commons of *England*, would deſtroy the Laws of the Land, and Liberties of the People; wherein, befides the Truſt of the whole; they themſelves in their own particulars, had ſo great an Intereſt of Honor, and Eſtate, that they hoped it would gain little Credit with any, that had the leaſt uſe of Reaſon, that ſuch, as muſt have ſo great a ſhare in the Miſery, ſhould take ſo much pains in the procuring thereof; and ſpend ſo much time, and run ſo many hazards to make themſelves Slaves, and to deſtroy the property of their Eſtates. But that they might give particular ſatisfaction to the ſeveral Imputations caſt upon them, they would take them in order, as they were laid upon them in that Meſſage.

"Firſt They were charged for the avowing that Act of Sir *John Hotham*; which was termed unparalleled, and a high, and unheard of Affront unto his Majeſty, and as if they needed not to have done it; he being able, as was alledged, to produce no ſuch Command of the Houſes of Parliament. They ſaid, although Sir *John Hotham* had not an Order, that did expreſs every Circumſtance of that caſe, yet he might have produced an Order of both Houſes, which did comprehend this Caſe, not only in the clear Intention,

" but in the very Words thereof; which they know-
" ing in their Confciences to be fo, and to be moſt
" neceſſary for the Safety of the Kingdom, they
" could not, but in Honor and Juſtice, avow that
" Act of His; which, they were confident, would
" appear to all the World to be ſo far from being
" an Affront to the King, that it would be found to
" have been an Act of great Loyalty to his Majeſty,
" and to his Kingdom.

" The next Charge upon them was, that inſtead
" of giving his Majeſty ſatisfaction, they publiſhed
" a Declaration concerning that buſineſs, as an Ap-
" peal to the People, and as if their intercourſe with
" his Majeſty, and for his ſatisfaction, were now
" to no more purpoſe; which courſe was alledged
" to be very unagreeable to the Modeſty and duty
" of former times, and not warrantable by any
" Precedents, but what Themſelves had made. They
" ſaid, if the Penner of that Meſſage had expected
" a while, or had not expected that two Houſes of
" Parliament (eſpecially burdened, as they were at
" that time, with ſo many preſſing, and urgent
" Affairs) ſhould have moved as faſt as himſelf, he
" would not have ſaid, that Declaration was inſtead
" of an Anſwer to his Majeſty; which they did
" deſpatch with all the ſpeed, and diligence they
" could, and had ſent it to his Majeſty by a Com-
" mittee of both Houſes; whereby it appeared, that
" they did it not upon that ground, that they thought
" it was no more to any purpoſe, to endeavour to
" give his Majeſty ſatisfaction.

" And as for the Duty and Modeſty of former

"times, from which they were said to have varied, and to want the Warrant of any Precedents therein, but what Themselves had made: If they had made any Precedents this Parliament, they had made them for Posterity, upon the same, or better grounds of Reason and Law, than those were upon, which their Predecessors first made for Them: And as some Precedents ought not to be rules for them to follow, so none could be limits to bound their Proceedings, which might, and must vary, according to the different condition of Times. And for that Particular, of setting forth Declarations for the satisfaction of the People, who had chosen, and intrusted them with all that was dearest to them: If there were no example for it, it was because there were never any Monsters before, that ever attempted to disaffect the People from a Parliament, or could ever harbour a thought that it might be effected. Were there ever such practices to poison the People with an ill apprehension of the Parliament? Were there ever such imputations, and scandals laid upon the Proceedings of both Houses? Were there ever so many, and so great breaches of Privilege of Parliament? Were there ever so many, and so desperate designs of force and violence against the Parliament, and the Members thereof? If they had Done more than ever their Ancestors had Done, they said, they had Suffered more than ever They had Suffered; and yet, in point of Modesty and Duty, they would not yield to the best of former times; and they would put that in issue, whether the highest,

OF THE REBELLION.

" and most unwarrantable Precedents of any of his
" Majesty's Predecessors, did not fall short, and much
" below, what had been done to them this Parlia-
" ment? And on the other side, whether, if they
" should make the highest Precedents of other Par-
" liaments their Patterns, there would be cause to
" complain of want of modesty, and duty in Them;
" when they had not so much as suffered such things
" to enter into their Thoughts, which all the world
" knew They put in Act?

" Another Charge which was laid very high upon
" them, and which were indeed a very great Crime
" if they were found guilty thereof, was, that by
" avowing that Act of Sir *John Hotham*, they did,
" in consequence, confound and destroy the title,
" and interest of all his Majesty's good Subjects to
" their Lands and Goods; and that, upon this
" ground; that his Majesty had the same Title to his
" Town of *Hull*, which any of his Subjects had to
" their Houses or Lands, and the same to his Ma-
" gazine and Munition there, that any Man had to
" his Money, Plate, or Jewels: And therefore,
" that they ought not to have been disposed of,
" without, or against his Consent, no more than the
" House, Land, Money, Plate, or Jewels of any Sub-
" ject ought to be, without, or against his Will.

" Here, they said, that was laid down for a
" Principle, which would indeed pull up the very
" foundation of the liberty, property, and interest
" of every Subject in particular, and of all the Subjects
" in general, if they should admit it for a truth, that
" his Majesty had the same right and title to his

"Towns, and to his Magazines (bought with the public Moneys, as they conceived that at *Hull* to have been) that every particular Man hath to his House, Lands, and Goods. For his Majesty's Towns were no more his own, than his Kingdom was his own; and his Kingdom was no more his own, than his People are his own; and if the King had a property in all his Towns, what would become of the Subjects' propriety in their Houses therein? and if He had a propriety in his Kingdom, what would become of the Subjects' property in their Lands throughout the Kingdom? or of their Liberties, if his Majesty had the same right in their Persons, that every Subject hath in his Lands, and Goods? and what would become of all the Subjects' interests in the Towns, and Forts of the Kingdom, and in the Kingdom itself, if his Majesty might sell, or give them away, or dispose of them at his pleasure, as a particular Man might do with his Goods? This erroneous Maxim being infused into Princes, that their Kingdoms are their own, and that they may do with them what they will, as if their Kingdoms were for Them, and not They for their Kingdoms, was, they said, the Root of all the Subjects' misery, and of the invading of their just Rights, and Liberties; whereas, indeed, they are only intrusted with their Kingdoms, and with their Towns, and with their People, and with the public Treasure of the Common-wealth, and whatsoever is bought therewith; and, by the known Law of this 'Kingdom; the very Jewels of the Crown are not the King's proper Goods, but

"are only intrusted to him, for the use and ornament
"thereof: As the Towns, Forts, Treasure, Maga-
"zines, Offices, and the People of the Kingdom, and
"the whole Kingdom itself is intrusted unto him, for
"the good, and safety, and best advantage thereof:
"and as this Trust is for the use of the Kingdom, so
"ought it to be managed by advice of the Houses of
"Parliament, whom the Kingdom hath trusted for that
"purpose; it being their duty to see it discharged
"according to the condition and true intent thereof;
"and as much as in them lies, by all possible means,
"to prevent the contrary; which, if it had been their
"chief care, and only aim, in the disposing of the
"Town and Magazine of *Hull* in such manner as they
"had done, they hoped it would appear clearly to
"all the world, that they had discharged their own
"Trust, and not invaded that of his Majesty, much
"less his Property; which, in that case, they could
"not do.

"But admitting his Majesty had indeed a Property
"in the Town and Magazine of *Hull*; who doubted
"but that a Parliament may dispose of any thing,
"wherein his Majesty, or any Subject hath a right,
"in such a way, as that the Kingdom may not be ex-
"posed to Hazard, or Danger thereby? Which was
"Their case, in the disposing of the Town and
"Magazine of *Hull*. And whereas his Majesty did
"allow this, and a greater power to a Parliament,
"but in that sense only, as he himself was a Part there-
"of; they appealed to every man's conscience, that
"had observed their proceedings, whether they
"disjoined his Majesty from his Parliament, who

"had in all humble ways sought his concurrence with them, as in that particular about *Hull*, and for the removal of the Magazine there, so also in all other things; or whether those evil Councils about him, had not separated him from his Parliament; not only in distance of place, but also in the discharge of the joint Trust with them, for the Peace and Safety of the Kingdom in that, and some other Particulars.

"They had given no occasion to his Majesty, they said to declare with so much earnestness his resolution, that he would not suffer either, or both Houses by their Votes, without, or against his Consent, to injoin any thing that was forbidden by the Law, or to forbid any thing that was injoined by the Law; for their Votes had done no such thing: And as they should be very tender of the Law (which they did acknowledge to be the safe-guard, and custody of all public and private Interests) so they would never allow a few private Persons about the King, nor his Majesty himself in his own Person, and out of his Courts, to be judge of the Law, and that contrary to the judgment of the highest Court of Judicature. In like manner, that His Majesty had not refused to consent to any thing, that might be for the Peace and Happiness of the Kingdom, they could not admit it in any other sense, but as his Majesty taketh the measure of what will be for the Peace and Happiness of his Kingdom, from some few ill affected Persons about him, contrary to the Advice, and Judgment of his great Council of Parliament. And because the

Advice

"Advice of both Houses of Parliament had through
"the suggestion of evil Counsellors, been so much
"undervalued of late, and so absolutely rejected and
"refused, they said, they held it fit to declare unto
"the Kingdom, whose Honor and Interest was so
"much concerned in it, what was the Privilege of
"the Great Council of Parliament herein; and what
"was the Obligation that lay upon the Kings of this
"Realm, to pass such Bills, as are offered to them
"by both Houses of Parliament, in the Name, and
"for the Good of the whole Kingdom, whereunto
"they stand engaged both in conscience, and justice,
"to give their Royal Assent: In Conscience, in
"regard of the Oath, that is, or ought to be taken by
"the Kings of this Realm at their Coronation, as
"well to confirm by their Royal Assent such good
"Laws, as the People shall chuse, and to remedy
"by Law such inconveniences, as the Kingdom may
"suffer; as to keep, and protect the Laws already in
"being; as may appear both by the Form of the Oath
"upon Record, and in Books of good Authority,
"and by the Statute of the 25. of *Edward* the III. en-
"titled the Statute of Provisors of Benefices; the
"Form of which Oath, and the Clause of the Statute
"that concerneth it, are as followeth:

   Rot Parliament. H. iv. *N* 17.

Forma juramenti soliti, & consueti præstari per
 Reges Angliæ in eorum Coronatione.

Servabis Ecclesiæ Dei, Cleroque, & Populo. pacem ex integro, & concordiam in Deo, secundum vires tuas?

   Respondebit, servabo.

VOL. IV.   G

BOOK V.

Facies fieri in omnibus judiciis tuis æquam, & rectam justitiam, & discretionem in misericordia & veritate, secundum vires tuas?

Respondebit, Faciam.

Concedis justas Leges, & consuetudines esse tenendas; & promittis per te eas esse protegendas, & ad honorem Dei corroborandas, quas Vulgus elegerit, secundum vires tuas?

Respondebit, Concedo & Promitto.

Adjicianturque prædictis Interrogationibus quæ justa fuerint, prænunciatisque omnibus, confirmet Rex se omnia servaturum, sacramento super Altare præstito, coram cunctis.

A Clause in the preamble of a Statute made the 25. Edw. III. entitled, the Statute of Provisors of Benefices.

Whereupon the said Commons have prayed our said Lord the King; That sith the Right of the Crown of *England*, and the Law of the said Realm is such, that upon the mischiefs and damages, which happen to this Realm, he ought, and is bound by his Oath, with the accord of his People in his Parliament, thereof to make Remedy and Law, and in removing the mischiefs, and damages which thereof ensue, that it may please him thereupon to ordain Remedy.

Our Lord the King seeing the mischiefs and damages before mentioned, and having regard to the Statute made in the time of his said Grandfather, and to the Causes contained in the same, which Statute holdeth always his force, and was never defeated, repealed, or annulled in any point, and by so much he is bound by his Oath to cause the same to be kept as the Law of his Realm, though that, by sufferance and negligence, it hath been sithence attempted to the contrary: Also having regard to the grievous complaints made to him by his People, in divers his Parliaments holden heretofore, willing to ordain remedy for the great damages, and mischiefs which have happened, and daily do happen, to the Church of *England* by the said Cause:

" Here, they said, the Lords, and Commons claim
" it directly as the Right of the Crown of *England*,
" and of the Law of the Land, and that the King is
" bound by his Oath, with the accord of his People
" in Parliament, to make remedy, and Law, upon
" the mischiefs and damages, which happen to this
" Realm; and the King doth not deny it, although
" he take occasion from a Statute formerly made by
" his Grandfather, which was laid as part of the
" grounds of this Petition, to fix his Answer upon
" another branch of his Oath, and pretermits that
" which is claimed by the Lords and Commons;
" which he would not have done, if it might have
" been excepted against.
" In Justice, they said, they are obliged there-
" unto, in respect of the Trust reposed in them;
" which is as well to preserve the Kingdom by the
" making new Laws, where there shall be need, as
" by observing of Laws already made; a Kingdom
" being, many times, as much exposed to ruin, for

"the want of a new Law, as by the violation of
"those that are in being: and this is so clear a Right,
"that, no doubt, his Majesty would acknowledge
"it to be as due to his People, as his Protection.
"But how far forth he was obliged to follow the
"judgment of his Parliament therein, that is the
"Question. And certainly, besides the words in
"the King's Oath, referring unto such Laws as the
"People shall chuse, as in such things which
"concern the public Weal and Good of the King-
"dom, They are the most proper judges, who are
"sent from the whole Kingdom for that very pur-
"pose; so they did not find, that since Laws have
"passed by way of Bills (which are read thrice in
"both Houses, and Committed; and every part,
"and circumstance of them fully weighed, and
"debated upon the Commitment, and afterwards
"passed in both Houses) that ever the Kings of this
"Realm did deny them, otherwise than is expressed
"in that usual Answer, *Le Roy Savisera*; which
"signifies rather a suspension, than a refusal of the
"Royal Assent. And in those other Laws, which
"are framed by way of Petitions of Right, the
"Houses of Parliament have taken themselves to be
"so far Judges of the Right claimed by them, that
"when the King's Answer hath not, in every point,
"been fully according to their desires, they have
"still insisted upon their claim, and never rested
"satisfied, till such time as they had an Answer
"according to their demand; as had been done in
"the late Petition of Right, and in former times upon
"the like occasion. And if the Parliament be judge

OF THE REBELLION.

"between the King and his People in the question
"of Right (as by the manner in the claim in Peti-
"tions of Right, and by judgments in Parliament,
"in cases of illegal impositions and taxes, and the
"like, it appears to be) why should they not be
"so also, in the question of the Common Good,
"and Necessity of the Kingdom, wherein the King-
"dom hath as clear a Right also to have the benefit,
"and remedy of Law, as in any thing whatsoever?
"And yet they did not deny, but that in private
"Bills, and also in public Acts of Grace, as Pardons,
"and the like Grants of Favor, his Majesty might
"have a greater latitude of Granting, or Denying,
"as he should think fit.

"All this considered, they said; they could not
"but wonder, that the Contriver, of that Message
"should conceive, the People of this Land to be so
"void of Common sense, as to enter into so deep
"a mistrust of those, whom they have, and his Ma-
"jesty ought to repose so great a Trust in, as to de-
"spair of any security in their private Estates, by
"Descents, Purchases, Assurances, or Conveyances;
"unless his Majesty should, by His Vote, prevent
"the prejudice, they might receive therein by the
"Votes of both Houses of Parliament; as if They,
"who are especially chosen, and intrusted for that
"purpose, and who Themselves must needs have so
"great a share in all Grievances of the Subject, had
"wholly cast off all care of the Subject's Good, and
"his Majesty had solely taken it up; and as if it could
"be imagined, that They should, by their Votes,
"overthrow the Rights of Descents, Purchases, or of

"any Conveyance or Assurance, in whose judgment
"the whole Kingdom hath placed all their particular
"interests, if any of them should be called in ques-
"tion, in any of those cases; and that (as not
"knowing where to place them, with greater se-
"curity) without any Appeal from Them to any
"other Person, or Court whatsoever.

"But indeed they were very much to seek, how
"the Case of *Hull* could concern Descents and Pur-
"chases, or Conveyances and Assurances; unless it
"were in procuring more security to Men in their
"Private interests, by the preservation of the Whole
"from confusion and destruction; and much less did
"they understand, how the Sovereign Power was
"resisted, and despised therein. Certainly no com-
"mand from his Majesty, and his high Court of
"Parliament (where the Sovereign Power resides)
"was disobeyed by Sir *John Hotham*; nor yet was his
"Majesty's Authority derived out of any other
"Court, nor by any legal Commission, or by any
"other way, wherein the Law had appointed his Ma-
"jesty's commands to be derived to his Subjects; and
"of what validity his Verbal Commands are, with-
"out any such Stamp of his Authority upon them,
"and against the Order of both Houses of Parlia-
"ment, and whether the not submitting thereunto,
"be a resisting and despising of the Sovereign Autho-
"rity, they would leave to all Men to judge, that do
"at all understand the Government of this Kingdom.

"They acknowledged that his Majesty had made
"many expressions of his Zeal, and Intentions against
"the desperate designs of the Papists; but yet it was

" also as true, that the Counsels, which had prevailed
" of late with him, had been little suitable to those
" Expressions, and Intentions. For what did more
" advance the open, and bloody design of the Papists
" in *Ireland* (whereon the secret Plots of the Papists
" here did, in all likelihood, depend) than his Ma-
" jesty's absenting himself, in that manner that he did,
" from his Parliament; and setting forth such sharp
" Invectives against them, notwithstanding all the
" humble Petitions, and other means, which his Par-
" liament had addressed unto him, for his return, and
" for his satisfaction concerning their proceedings?
" And what was more likely to give a rise to the de-
" signs of the Papists (whereof there were so many in
" the North, near to the Town of *Hull*) and of other
" malignant, and ill affected Persons (which were
" ready to join with them) or to the attempts of Fo-
" reigners from abroad, than the continuing of that
" great Magazine at *Hull*, at this time, and contrary
" to the desire and advice of both Houses of Parlia-
" ment? So that they had too much cause to believe,
" that the Papists had still some way and means,
" whereby they had influence upon his Majesty's
" Counsels for their own advantage.

" For the Malignant Party, they said, his Majesty
" needed not a definition of the Law, nor yet a
" more full Character of them from both Houses of
" Parliament, for to find them out, if he would
" please only to apply the Character, that Him-
" self had made of them, to those, unto whom
" it doth properly and truly belong. Who are so
" much disaffected to the Peace of the Kingdom,

"as they that endeavour to disaffect his Majesty from the Houses of Parliament, and persuade him to be at such a distance from them, both in place and affection? Who are more disaffected to the Government of the Kingdom, than such as lead his Majesty away from hearkening to his Parliament, which, by the constitution of the Kingdom, is his greatest and best Council; and persuade him to follow the malicious Counsels of some private Men, in opposing and contradicting the wholesome Advices, and just Proceedings of that his most faithful Council, and highest Court? Who are they, that not only neglect and despise, but labor to undermine the Law under color of maintaining it, but they that endeavour to destroy the Fountain, and Conservatory of the Law, which is the Parliament? And Who are they that set up other Rules for themselves to walk by, than such as were according to Law, but they that will make other Judges of the Law than the Law hath appointed; and so dispense with their Obedience to that, which the Law calleth Authority, and to Their determinations and resolutions, to whom the judgment doth appertain by Law? For, when private Persons shall make the Law to be their Rule according to their own understanding, contrary to the Judgment of those that are the competent Judges thereof, they set up unto themselves other Rules than the Law doth acknowledge. Who those Persons were, none knew better than his Majesty himself: And if he would please to take all possible caution of them, as destructive to the Common-wealth and Himself, and would

"remove them from about him, it would be the most
"effectual means to compose all the Distractions, and
"to cure the Distempers of the Kingdom.

"For the Lord *Digby's* Letter, they said, they
"did not make mention of it as a ground to hinder
"his Majesty from visiting his own Fort; but they
"appealed to the judgment of any indifferent Man,
"that should read that Letter, and compare it with
"the posture that his Majesty then did, and still
"doth, stand in towards the Parliament, and with
"the circumstances of that late Action of his Ma-
"jesty's going to *Hull*, whether the advisers to that
"Journey intended only a Visit of that Fort, and
"Magazine?

"As to the ways and overtures of Accommoda-
"tion, and the Message of the twentieth of *January*
"last, so often pressed, but still in vain, as was
"alledged: Their Answer was, That although so
"often as that Message of the twentieth of *January*
"had been pressed, so often had their Privileges
"been clearly infringed, that a way and method of
"proceedings should be prescribed to them; as well
"for the settling of his Majesty's Revenue, as for
"the presenting of their own Desires (a thing which
"in former Parliaments had always been excepted
"against, as a breach of Privilege) yet, in respect to
"the matter contained in that Message, and out of
"their earnest desire to beget a good understanding
"between his Majesty and them, they swallowed
"down all matters of Circumstance; and had ere
"that time presented the chief of their desires to his
"Majesty, had they not been interrupted with con-

"tinual Denials, even of those things that were necessary for their present Security, and Subsistence; and had not those Denials been followed with perpetual Invectives against Them, and their Proceedings; and had not those Invectives been heaped upon them so thick one after another (who were in a manner already taken up wholly with the pressing Affairs of this Kingdom, and of the Kingdom of *Ireland*) that as they had little encouragement from thence, to hope for any good Answers to their Desires, so they had not so much time left them to perfect them in such a manner, as to offer them to his Majesty.

"They confessed it to be a Resolution most worthy of a Prince, and of his Majesty, to shut his Ears against any that would incline him to a Civil War; and to abhor the very apprehension of it. But they could not believe that mind to have been in Them, that came with his Majesty to the House of Commons, or in Them that accompanied his Majesty to *Hampton*-Court, and appeared in a Warlike manner at *Kingston* upon *Thames*; or in divers of Them, who followed his Majesty lately to *Hull*; or in Them, who after drew their Swords in *York*, demanding, *Who would be for the King?* nor in Them that advised his Majesty to declare Sir *John Hotham* a Traytor, before the Message was sent concerning that business to the Parliament, or to make Propositions to the Gentlemen of the County of *York* to assist his Majesty to proceed against him in a way of Force, before he had, or possibly could receive an Answer from

"the Parliament, to whom he had sent to demand
"Justice of them against Sir *John Hotham* for that
"Fact: and if those Malignant Spirits should ever
"force them to defend their Religion, the King-
"dom, the Privileges of Parliament, and the Rights,
"and Liberties of the Subjects, with their Swords;
"the Blood, and Destruction that should ensue there-
"upon, must be wholly cast upon Their Account;
"God, and their own Consciences told them, that
"They were clear; and they doubted not, but God,
"and the whole World would clear them therein.

"For Captain *Leg*, they had not said that he was
"accused, or that there was any Charge against him,
"for the bringing up of the Army; but that he
"was employed in that Business. And for that con-
"cerning the Earl of *New-Castle*, mentioned by his
"Majesty, which was said to have been asked long
"since, and that it was not easy to be Answered:
"They conceived it was a Question of more diffi-
"culty, and harder to be Answered, why, when
"his Majesty held it necessary, upon the same
"grounds that first moved from the Houses of Par-
"liament, that a Governor should be placed in that
"Town, Sir *John Hotham*, a Gentleman of known
"Fortune and Integrity, and a Person of whom
"both Houses of Parliament had expressed their Con-
"fidence, should be refused by his Majesty; and
"the Earl of *New-Castle* (who, by the way, was so
"far named in the business of bringing up the Army,
"that although there was not ground enough for a
"Judicial Proceeding, yet there was ground of Sus-
"picion; at least his Reputation was not left so

"unblemished thereby, as that he should be thought
"the fittest Man in *England* for that Employment of
"*Hull*) should be sent down, in a private way, from
"his Majesty to take upon him that Government?
"And why he should disguise himself under another
"Name, when he came thither, as he did? But
"whosoever should consider, together with those
"circumstances, that of the Time when Sir *John*
"*Hotham* was appointed, by both Houses of Par-
"liament, to take upon him that Employment,
"which was presently after his Majesty's coming to
"the House of Commons, and upon the retiring
"himself to *Hampton*-Court, and the Lord *Digby's*
"assembling of Cavaliers at *Kingston* upon *Thames*,
"would find reason enough, why that Town of *Hull*
"should be committed rather to Sir *John Hotham*,
"by the Authority of both Houses of Parliament,
"than to the Earl of *New-Castle*, sent from his Ma-
"jesty in that manner that he was. And for the
"Power, that Sir *John Hotham* had from the two
"Houses of Parliament, the better it was known and
"understood, they were confident the more it would
"be approved and justified: and as they did not con-
"ceive, that his Majesty's refusal to have that Maga-
"zine removed, could give any advantage against him
"to have it taken from him; and as no such thing
"was done, so they could not conceive, for what
"other Reason any should counsel his Majesty, not
"to suffer it to be removed, upon the desire of both
"Houses of Parliament; except it were, that they had
"an intention to make use of it against Them.

"They said, they did not except against those

" that presented a Petition to his Majesty at *York*, for
" the continuance of the Magazine at *Hull*, in respect
" of their Condition, or in respect of their Number;
" because they were Mean Persons, or because they
" were Few; but because they being but a few, and
" there being so many more in the County of as
" good Quality as themselves (who had, by their Pe-
" tition to his Majesty, disavowed that Act of theirs)
" that they should take upon them the Style of all
" the Gentry, and Inhabitants of that County; and,
" under that Title, should presume to interpose their
" Advice contrary to the Votes of both Houses of
" Parliament: And, if it could be made to appear,
" that any of those Petitions, that are said to have
" been presented to the Houses of Parliament, and
" to have been of a strange nature, were of such
" a nature as that, They were confident, that they
" were never received with their Consent, and
" Approbation.

" Whether there was an Intention to deprive Sir
" *John Hotham* of his Life, if his Majesty had been
" admitted into *Hull*; and whether the Information
" were such, as that he had ground to believe it,
" they would not bring into question; for that was
" not, nor ought to have been, the ground for doing
" what he did: Neither was the Number of his Ma-
" jesty's Attendants, for being more or fewer, much
" considerable in this Case; for although it were
" true, that if his Majesty had entered with twenty
" Horse only, he might happily have found means for
" to have forced the Entrance of the rest of his Train;
" who, being once in the Town, would not have
" been long without Arms; yet That was not the

"Ground, upon which Sir *John Hotham* was to proceed; but upon the Admittance of the King into the Town at all, so as to deliver up the Town and Magazine unto him, and to whomsoever he should give the Command thereof, without the Knowledge and Consent of both Houses of Parliament, by whom he was intrusted to the contrary: and his Majesty having declared, that to be his intention concerning the Town, in a Message that he sent to the Parliament, not long before he went to *Hull*; saying, that he did not doubt, but that Town should be delivered up to him, whensoever he pleased, as supposing it to be kept against him; and in like manner concerning his Magazine, in his Message of the 24th of *April*, wherein it is expressed, that his Majesty went thither, with a purpose to take into his hands the Magazine, and to dispose of it in such manner, as he should think fit: Upon those Terms, Sir *John Hotham* could not have admitted his Majesty, and have made good his Trust to the Parliament, though his Majesty would have entered alone, without any Attendants at all of his own, or of the Prince or Duke, his Sons; which they did not wish to be less, than they were, in their Number, but could heartily wish that they were generally better in their Condition.

"In the close of that Message, his Majesty stated the Case of *Hull*; and thereupon inferred, that the Act of Sir *John Hotham* was levying War against the King; and, consequently, that it was no less than High-Treason, by the Letter of the Statute of the 25. *Edw.* III. *ch.* 2. unless the Sense of

"that Statute were very far differing from the Letter
"thereof.

"In the stating of that Case, they said, divers
"Particulars might be observed, wherein it was
"not rightly stated: As,

1. "That his Majesty's going to *Hull*, was only
"an endeavour to Visit a Town, and Fort of his:
"whereas it was indeed to Possess himself of the
"Town, and Magazine there, and to dispose of
"them, as he himself should think good, without,
"and contrary to the Advice and Orders of both
"Houses of Parliament; as did clearly appear by
"his Majesty's own Declaration of his Intentions
"therein, by his Messages to both Houses, imme-
"diately before, and after that Journey. Nor could
"they believe, that any Man, who should consider
"the circumstances of that Journey to *Hull*, could
"think, that his Majesty would have gone thither
"at that time, and in that posture, that he was
"pleased to put himself in towards the Parliament,
"if he had intended only a Visit of the Town and
"Magazine.

2. "It was said to be his Majesty's own Town,
"and his own Magazine, which being understood
"in that sense, as was before expressed, as if his
"Majesty had a private Interest of Propriety therein,
"they could not admit it to be so.

3. "Which was the main Point of all, Sir *John
"Hotham* was said to have shut the Gates against
"his Majesty, and to have made resistance with
"Armed Men, in defiance of his Majesty; whereas
"it was indeed in obedience to his Majesty, and his

"Authority, and for his Service, and the Service of
"the Kingdom; for which use only, all that Interest
"is, that the King hath in the Town; and it is no
"further his to dispose of, than he useth it for that
"end: And Sir *John Hotham* being Commanded to
"keep the Town and Magazine, for his Majesty
"and the Kingdom, and not to deliver them up, but
"by his Majesty's Authority signified by both
"Houses of Parliament, all that was to be understood
"by those expressions, of his denying, and opposing
"his Majesty's entrance, and telling him in plain
"terms, that he should not come in, was only this,
"that he humbly desired his Majesty to forbear his
"entrance, till he might acquaint the Parliament;
"and that his Authority might come signified to him
"by both Houses of Parliament, according to the
"Trust reposed in him. And certainly, if the Letter
"of the Statute of the 25. *Edw.* III. *ch.* 2. be thought
"to import this, That no War can be Levied against
"the King, but what is directed, and intended
"against his Person, or that every Levying of Forces
"for the defence of the King's Authority, and of his
"Kingdom, against the Personal Commands of the
"King opposed thereunto, though accompanied
"with his Presence, is Levying War against the King,
"it is very far from the Sense of that Statute; and so
"much the Statute itself speaks (besides the Autho-
"rity of Book-Cases; Precedents of divers Traytors
"condemned upon that interpretation thereof) For if
"the Clause of Levying of War had been meant only
"against the King's Person, what need had there
"been thereof after the other branch of Treason,

in

"in the same Statute, of compassing the King's
" Death, which should necessarily have implied this?
" And because the former Clause doth imply this, it
" seems not all to be intended in this latter branch;
" but only the Levying of War against the King,
" that is, against his Laws and Authority: And the
" Levying of War against his Laws and Authority,
" though not against his Person, is Levying War
" against the King; but the Levying of Force against
" his Personal Commands, though accompanied
" with his Presence, and not against his Laws and
" Authority, but in the maintenance thereof, is no
" Levying of War against the King, but for him.

"Here was then, they said, their Case, In a time
" of so many successive Plots, and Designs of Force
" against the Parliament, and the Kingdom; in a
" time of probable Invasion from abroad, and that
" to begin at *Hull*, and to take the opportunity of
" seizing upon so great a Magazine there; in a time
" of so great distance and alienation of his Majesty's
" Affection from his Parliament (and in Them from
" his Kingdom, which they represent) by the wicked
" suggestions of a few Malignant Persons, by whose
" mischievous Counsels he was wholly led away
" from his Parliament, and their faithful Advices
" and Counsels: In such a time, the Lords and Com-
" mons in Parliament command Sir *John Hotham*, to
" draw in some of the Trained bands of the parts
" adjacent to the Town of *Hull*, for the securing that
" Town and Magazine for the Service of his Majesty,
" and of the Kingdom: of the safety whereof there is
" a higher Trust reposed in Them, than any where

"else; and They are the proper Judges of the danger thereof.

"This Town and Magazine being intrusted to Sir *John Hotham* with express Order not to deliver them up, but by the King's Authority signified by both Houses of Parliament; his Majesty, contrary to the Advice and Directions of both Houses of Parliament, without the Authority of any Court, or any Legal way, wherein the Law appoints the King to speak and command, accompanied with the same evil Council about him that he had before, by a Verbal command requires Sir *John Hotham* to admit him into the Town, that he might dispose of It, and of the Magazine there, according to his own, or rather according to the pleasure of those evil Counsellors, who are still in so much credit about him; in like manner as the Lord *Digby* had continual recourse unto, and countenance from, the Queen's Majesty in *Holland*; by which means he had opportunity still to communicate his Trayterous conceptions, and suggestions to both their Majesties; such as those were concerning his Majesty's retiring to a place of Strength, and Declaring himself, and his own advancing his Majesty's Service in such a way beyond the Seas, and after that resorting to his Majesty in such a place of strength; and divers other things of that nature, contained in his Letter to the Queen's Majesty, and to Sir *Lewis Dives*; a Person, that had not the least part in this late business of *Hull*, and was presently despatched away into *Holland*, soon after his Majesty's return from *Hull*; for what Purpose, they left the world to judge.

"Upon the refusal of Sir *John Hotham* to admit his Majesty into *Hull*, presently, without any due process of Law, before his Majesty had sent up the narration of this Fact to the Parliament, he was proclaimed Traytor; and yet it was said, that therein was no violation of the Subjects' Rights, nor any breach of the Law, nor of the Privilege of Parliament, though Sir *John Hotham* be a Member of the House of Commons; and that his Majesty must have better reason, than bare Votes, to believe the contrary; although the Votes of the Lords and Commons in Parliament, being the Great Council of the Kingdom, are the reason of the King, and of the Kingdom: yet these Votes, they said, did not want clear, and apparent reason for them; for if the solemn proclaiming him a Traytor signify any thing, it puts a Man, and all those that any way aid, assist, or adhere unto him, in the same condition of Traytors; and draws upon him all the consequences of Treason: And if that might be done by Law, without due process of Law, the Subject hath a very poor defence of the Law; and a very small, if any proportion of Liberty thereby. And it is as little satisfaction to a Man, that shall be exposed to such Penalties, by that Declaration of him to be Traytor, to say, he shall have a Legal Trial afterwards, as it is to condemn a Man first, and try him afterwards. And if there could be a necessity for any such proclaiming a Man a Traytor without due process of Law, yet there was none in this case; for his Majesty might as well have expected the judgment of Parliament (which was "the right way) as he had leisure to send to them to "demand justice against Sir *John Hotham*. And the "breach of Privilege of Parliament was as clear in "this Case, as the subversion of the Subjects' Com- "mon right: For, though the Privileges of Parlia- "ment, do not extend to those Cases, mentioned in "the Declaration, of Treason, Felony, and Breach "of Peace, so as to exempt the Members of Parlia- "ment from punishment, nor from all manner of "Process and Trial, as it doth in other Cases; yet it "doth Privilege them in the Way, and Method of "their Trial and Punishment; and that the Parlia- "ment should have the Cause first brought before "them, that they may judge of the Fact, and of the "grounds of the Accusation; and how far forth the "manner of their Trial may concern, or not con- "cern the Privilege of Parliament. Otherwise it "would be in the power, not only of his Majesty, "but of every Private man, under pretensions of "Treasons, or those other Crimes, to take any Man "from his Service in Parliament; and so as many one "after another as he pleaseth; and, consequently, to "make a Parliament what he will, when he will; "which would be a breach of so Essential a Privilege "of Parliament, as that the very Being thereof de- "pends upon it. And therefore they no ways doub- "ted but every One, that had taken the Protestation, "would, according to his Solemn Vow, and Oath, "defend it with his Life, and Fortune. Neither did "the sitting of a Parliament suspend all, or any Law, "in maintaining that Law which upholds the Privi- "lege of Parliament: which upholds the Parliament; "which upholds the Kingdom. And they were so far

" from believing, that his Majesty was the only Per-
" son against whom Treason could Not be commit-
" ted, that, in some sense, they acknowledged he
" was the only Person against whom it Could be
" committed; that is, as he is King: and that Treason
" which is against the Kingdom, is more against the
" King, than that which is against his Person; because
" he is King: For that very Treason is not Treason,
" as it is against him as a Man, but as a man that is a
" King; and as he hath relation to the Kingdom, and
" stands as a Person intrusted with the Kingdom,
" and discharging that Trust.

" Now, they said, the Case was truly stated, and
" all the world might judge where the Fault was;
" although they must avow, that there could be no
" competent Judge of this, or any the like Case, but
" a Parliament. And they were as confident, that his
" Majesty should never have cause to resort to any
" other Court, or Course, for the vindication of his
" just Privileges, and for the recovery and mainte-
" nance of his known, and undoubted Rights, if
" there should be any Invasion, or Violation thereof,
" than to his high Court of Parliament: And, in case
" those wicked Counsellors about him, should drive
" him into any other Course from, and against his Par-
" liament, whatever his Majesty's expressions, and in-
" tentions were, they should appeal to all men's Con-
" sciences; and desire, that they would lay their hands
" upon their hearts, and think with themselves whe-
" ther such Persons, as had of late, and still did resort
" unto his Majesty, and had his ear, and favor most,
" either had been, or were more Zealous Assertors of

"the true Proteſtant Profeſſion (although they be-
"lieved they were more earneſt in the Proteſtant
"Profeſſion, than in the Proteſtant Religion) or the
"Law of the Land, the Liberty of the Subject, and
"the Privileges of the Parliament, than the Members
"of both Houſes of Parliament; who were inſinuated
"to be Deſerters, if not the Deſtroyers of them: And
"whether if they could maſter this Parliament by
"force, they would not hold up the ſame power to
"deprive us of all Parliaments; which are the Ground,
"and Pillar of the Subjects' Liberty, and that which
"only maketh *England* a free Monarchy.

"For the Order of Aſſiſtance to the Committee of
"both Houſes; as they had no Directions or Inſtruc-
"tions, but what had the Laws for their Limits,
"and the Safety of the Land for their Ends, ſo they
"doubted not but all perſons mentioned in that
"Order, and all his Majeſty's good Subjects, would
"yield obedience to his Majeſty's Authority, ſignifi-
"ed therein by both Houſes of Parliament. And that
"all Men might the better know their duty in
"matters of that nature, and upon how ſure a ground
"They go, that follow the judgment of Parliament
"for their Guide, they wiſhed them judiciouſly to
"conſider the true meaning, and ground of that
"Statute made in the elventh Year of King H. VII. ch. 1.
"which was printed at large in the end of his Ma-
"jeſty's Meſſage of the fourth of *May*: That Statute
"provides, that none who ſhall attend upon the
"King, and do him true Service, ſhould be attaint-
"ed, or forfeit any thing. What was the Scope
"of that Statute? To provide that Men ſhould not

" suffer as Traytors, for serving the King in his Wars
" according to the duty of their Allegiance? If this
" had been all, it had been a very needless, and ridi-
" culous Statute. Was it then intended (as They
" seemed to take the meaning of it to be, that caused
" it to be printed after his Majesty's Message) that
" They should be free from all Crime and Penalty,
" that should follow the King, and serve him in War
" in any case whatsoever; whether it were for, or
" against the Kingdom, and the Laws thereof? That
" could not be; for that could not stand with the duty
" of their Allegiance; which, in the beginning of the
" Statute, was expressed to be to serve the King for
" the time being in his Wars, for the defence of Him,
" and the Land; and therefore if it be against the Land
" (as it cannot be understood to be otherwise, if it
" be against the Parliament, the Representative body
" of the kingdom) it is a declining from the duty of
" Allegiance; which this Statute supposed may be
" done, though Men should follow the King's Person
" in the War: Otherwise there had been no need of
" such a Proviso in the end of the Statute, that none
" should take the benefit thereby, that should
" decline from their Allegiance. That therefore
" which is the principal Verb in this Statute is, The
" serving of the King for the time being; which could
" not be meant of *Perkin Warbeck*, or any that should
" call himself King; but such a One, as whatever his
" Title might prove, either in Himself, or in his An-
" cestors, should be received, and acknowledged for
" such by the Kingdom; the Consent whereof cannot
" be discerned but by Parliament; the Act whereof

"is the Act of the whole Kingdom, by the Personal
"Suffrage of the Peers, and the delegate Consent of
"all the Commons of *England*.

"And *Henry* the VII. a wise King considering that
"what was the case of *Rich.* III. his Predecessor,
"might, by chance of battle, be his own; and that
"he might at once, by such a Statute as this, satisfy
"such, as had served his Predecessor in his Wars,
"and also secure those, which should serve Him,
"who might otherwise fear to serve him in the
"Wars; lest, by chance of Battle, That might
"happen to him also (if a Duke of *York* had set up a
"Title against him) which had happened to his Pre-
"decessor, he procured this Statute to be made, That
"no Man should be accounted a Traytor for serving
"the King, in his Wars, for the time being, that is,
"which was for the present allowed, and received
"by the Parliament in behalf of the Kingdom: And,
"as it is truly suggested in the preamble of the
"Statute, it is not agreeable to Reason or Conscience,
"that it should be otherwise; seeing Men should be
"put upon an Impossibility of knowing their Duty,
"if the judgment of the highest Court should not be
"a Rule, and Guide to them. And if the judgment
"thereof should be followed, where the Question is,
"who is King? much more, what is the best Service
"of the King, and Kingdom? And therefore those,
"who should guide themselves by the judgment of
"Parliament ought, whatever happen, to be secure
"and free from all Account and Penalties, upon
"the Grounds and Equity of this very Statute.

"They said, they would conclude, that although

" thofe wicked Counfellors about his Majefty, had
" prefumed, under his Majefty's Name, to put that
" difhonor, and affront upon both Houfes of Parlia-
" ment; and to make Them the countenancers of
" Treafon, enough to have diffolved all the bands,
" and finews of the confidence between his Majefty,
" and his Parliament (of whom the Maxim of the
" Law is, that a difhonorable thing ought not to be
" imagined of them) yet they doubted not, but it
" fhould, in the end, appear to all the world, that
" their endeavours had been moft hearty and fincere,
" for the maintenance of the true Proteftant Reli-
" gion; the King's juft Prerogative; the Laws, and
" Liberties, of the Land; and the Privileges of Parlia-
" ment: in which endeavours, by the Grace of God,
" they would ftill perfift, though they fhould perifh
" in the work ; which if it fhould be, it was much to
" be feared, that Religion, Laws, Liberties, and Par-
" liaments, would not be long-lived after them."

This Declaration wrought more upon the minds of Men, than all that they had done: for the bufinefs at *Hull* was, by very many, thought to be done before projected; and the Argument of the Militia to be entered upon at firft in paffion, and afterwards purfued with that vehemence, infenfibly, by being engaged, and that both extravagances had fo much weighed down the King's Trefpaffes, in coming to the Houfe and accufing the Members, that a reafonable agreement would have been the fooner confented to on all hands. But when, by this Declaration, they faw Foundations laid, upon which not only what had been already done, would be well

BOOK V.

justified, but whatsoever they should, hereafter, find convenient to second what was already done; and that not only the King, but the Regal Power was either suppressed, or deposited in other hands; the irregularity, and monstrousness of which Principles found little opposition or resistance, even for the Irregularity, and Monstrousness: Very many thought it as unsafe to be present at those Consultations, as to consent to the Conclusions; and so great Numbers of the Members of both Houses absenting themselves; and many, especially of the House of Peers resorted to his Majesty at *York*. So that, in the Debates of the highest consequence, there was not usually present, in the House of Commons, the fifth part of their just Numbers; and, very often, not above a Dozen or Thirteen, in the House of Peers. In the mean time the King had a full Court, and received all Comers with great clemency, and grace; calling always all the Peers to Council, and communicating with them all such Declarations, as he thought fit to publish in Answer to those of the Parliament; and all Messages, and whatever else was necessary to be done for the improvement of his condition: And, having now the Great Seal with him, issued such Proclamations, as were seasonable for the preservation of the Peace of the Kingdom. First he published a Declaration in Answer to that of the nineteenth of *May*, in which his Majesty said,

His Majesty's Answer to the Declaration of the 19 of May.

" That if he could be weary of taking any pains
" for the satisfaction of his People, and to undeceive
" them of those specious, mischievous infusions,
" which were daily instilled into them to shake, and

"corrupt their Loyalty, and Affection to his Majesty
"and his Government, after so full, and ample Decla-
"ration of himself and Intentions, and so fair and
"satisfactory Answers to all such matters as had been
"objected to him, by a Major part present of both
"Houses of Parliament, He might well give over
"that labor of his Pen; and sit still, till it should
"please God to enlighten the affections, and under-
"standings of his good Subjects on his behalf (which
"he doubted not, but that, in His good Time, he
"would do) that they might see His sufferings were
"Their sufferings: but since, instead of applying
"themselves to the method, proposed by his Majesty,
"of making such solid particular Propositions, as
"might establish a good understanding between
"them, or of following the advice of his Council of
"*Scotland* (with whom they communicated their
"affairs) in forbearing all means that might make the
"breach wider, and the wound deeper; they had
"chosen to pursue his Majesty with new Reproaches,
"or rather to continue and improve the old, by ad-
"ding, and varying little Circumstances and Lan-
"guage, in matters formerly urged by them, and fully
"Answered by his Majesty, He had prevailed with
"himself, upon very mature and particular considera-
"tion of it, to Answer the late printed Book enti-
"tled a Declaration, or Remonstrance of the Lords
"and Commons, which was ordered, the nineteenth
"of *May* last, to be printed and published; hoping
"then, that they would put his Majesty to no more of
"that trouble, but that That should have been the last
"of such a Nature they would have communicated to

"his People; and that they would not, as they had done since, have thought fit to assault him with a newer Declaration, indeed of a very New nature, and Learning; which should have another Answer: and he doubted not, but that his good Subjects would, in short time, be so well instructed in the differences, and mistakings between them, that they would plainly discern, without resigning their reason and understanding to His Perogative, or the Infallibility of a now Major part of both Houses of Parliament (infected by a few Malignant Spirits) where the Fault was.

"His Majesty said, though he should, with all humility and alacrity, be always forward to acknowledge the Infinite Mercy, and Providence of Almighty God, vouchsafed, so many several ways, to Himself and this Nation; yet since God himself doth not allow, that we should fancy, and create dangers to ourselves, that we might manifest, and publish his Mercy in our Deliverance; he must profess, that he did not know those Deliverances, mentioned in the beginning of that Declaration, from so many wicked Plots and Designs, since the beginning of this Parliament, which, if they had taken effect, would have brought ruin and destruction upon this Kingdom His Majesty well knew the great labor and skill, which had been used to amuse, and affright his good Subjects with fears, and apprehensions of Plots and Conspiracies; the several Pamphlets published, and Letters scattered up and down, full of such ridiculous, contemptible animadversions to that purpose,

"as (though they found, for what end God knows,
"very unusual countenance) no Sober man would
"be moved with them. But, he muſt confeſs, he
"had never been able to inform himſelf of any ſuch
"pernicious, formed deſign againſt the Peace of the
"Kingdom, ſince the beginning of this Parliament,
"as was mentioned in that Declaration, or which
"might be any Warrant to thoſe great Fears, both
"Houſes of Parliament ſeemed to be tranſported
"with; but he had great reaſon to believe, that
"more miſchief and danger had been raiſed and be-
"gotten, to the diſturbance of the Kingdom, than
"cu:ed and prevented, by thoſe Fears, and Jea-
"louſies. And therefore, however the rumor,
"and diſcourſe of Plots and Conſpiracies, might
"have been neceſſary to the deſigns of particular
"Men, they ſhould do well not to pay any falſe
"Devotions to Almighty God, who diſcerns whe-
"ther our dangers are real, or pretended.

"For the bringing up of the Army to *London*,
"as his Majeſty had heretofore, by no other direc-
"tion than the teſtimony of a good Conſcience,
"called God to Witneſs that he never had, or knew
"of, any ſuch Reſolution; ſo he ſaid, upon the
"view of the Depoſitions now publiſhed with that
"Declaration, it was not evident to his Majeſty,
"that there was ever ſuch a Deſign; unleſs every
"looſe Diſcourſe, or Argument, be evidence enough
"of a Deſign; And it was apparent, that what had
"been ſaid of it, was near three Months before the
"Diſcovery to both Houſes of Parliament; ſo that
"if there were any danger threatened that way,

"it vanished without any resistance or prevention
"by the Wisdom, Power, or Authority of Them.
"It seemed the intention of that Declaration,
"whatsoever other End it had, was to Answer a
"Declaration, they had received from his Majesty,
"in Answer to that which was presented to his
"Majesty at *New-Market*, the ninth of *March* last;
"and likewise his Answer to the Petition of both
"Houses, presented to him at *York*, the 26th of *March*:
"But, before it fell upon any Particular of his Ma-
"jesty's Declaration or Answer, it complained that
"the Heads of the Malignant Party had, with much
"Art and Industry, advised him to suffer divers
"unjust Scandals, and Imputations upon the Parlia-
"ment, to be published in His Name, whereby
"they might make it odious to the People, and, by
"their help, destroy it: but not instancing in any
"one Scandal, or Imputation, so published by his
"Majesty, he was, he said, still to seek for the
"Heads of that Malignant Party. But his good Sub-
"jects would easily understand, that if he were
"guilty of that aspersion, he must not only be active
"in raising the Scandal, but passive in the mischief
"begotten by that Scandal, his Majesty being an
"Essential part of the Parliament; and he hoped the
"just Defence of Himself and his Authority, and the
"necessary Vindication of his Innocence and Justice,
"from the imputations laid on him, by a Major part
"then present of either or both Houses, should no
"more be called a Scandal upon the Parliament, than
"the Opinion of such a part be reputed an Act of
"Parliament: And he hoped his good Subjects would

" not be long mifled, by that common expreffion
" in all the Declarations, wherein they ufurp the
" word Parliament, and apply it to countenance any
" Refolution or Vote fome few had a mind to make,
" by calling it the Refolution of Parliament; which
" could never be without his Majefty's Confent;
" neither could the Vote of either or both Houfes
" make a greater alteration in the Laws of the King-
" dom (fo folemnly made by the advice of their Pre-
" deceffors, with the Concurrence of his Majefty
" and his Anceftors) either by commanding, or in-
" hibiting any thing (befides the known rule of the
" Law) than his fingle Direction or Mandate could
" do, to which he did not afcribe that Authority.

" But that Declaration informed the People, that
" the Malignant Party had drawn his Majefty into
" the Northern Parts, far from his Parliament. It
" might, his Majefty faid, more truly and properly
" have faid, that it had Driven, than Drawn him
" thither; for, he confeffed, his Journey thither (for
" which he had no other reafon to be forry, than
" with reference to the Caufe of it) was only forced
" upon him, by the true Malignant Party; which
" contrived and countenanced thofe barbarous Tu-
" mults, and other feditious Circumftances, of which
" he had fo often complained, and hereafter fhould
" fay more; and which indeed threatened fo much
" danger to his Perfon, and laid fo much Scandal upon
" the Privilege, and Dignity of Parliament, that he
" wondered it could be mentioned without blufhes
" or indignation: But of that, anon: But why the
" Malignant Party fhould be charged with the caufing

"a Press to be transported to *York*, his Majesty said,
"he could not imagine; neither had any Papers or
"Writings issued from thence, to His knowledge,
"but what had been extorted from him by such
"Provocations, as had not been before offered to a
"King. And, no doubt, it would appear a most tri-
"vial, and fond Exception, when all Presses were
"open to vent whatsoever they thought fit to say to
"the People (a thing unwarranted by former custom)
"that his Majesty should not make use of all Lawful
"means, to publish his just, and necessary Answers
"thereunto. As for the Authority of the Great Seal
"(though he did not know that it had been necef-
"sary to things of that nature) the same should be
"more frequently used hereafter, as occasion should
"require; to which he made no doubt, but the
"greater, and better part of his Privy-Council would
"concur; and whose advice he was resolved to fol-
"low, as far as it should be agreeable to the Good,
"and Welfare of the Kingdom.

"Before that Declaration vouchsafed to insist upon
"any Particulars, it was pleased to censure both his
"Majesty's Declaration and Answer to be filled with
"harsh Censures, and causeless Charges upon the Par-
"liament (still misapplying the word Parliament to
"the Vote of both Houses) concerning which they
"resolve to give satisfaction to the Kingdom, since
"they found it very difficult to satisfy his Majesty.
"If, as in the usage of the word Parliament, they
"had left his Majesty out of their thoughts; so by the
"word Kingdom, they intended to exclude all his
"People who were not within their Walls (for that

was

" was grown another Phrase of the time, the Vote of
" the Major part of both Houses, and sometimes of one,
" was now called the Resolution of the whole King-
" dom) his Majesty believed, it might not be hard to
" give satisfaction to Themselves; otherwise he was
" confident (and, he said, his confidence proceeded.
" from the uprightness of his own Conscience) they
" would never be able so to sever the Affections of his
" Majesty and his Kingdom, that what could not be
" satisfaction to the One, should be to the Other:
" Neither would the Style of Humble, and Faithful,
" and telling his Majesty, that they will make him a
" Great and Glorious King, in their Petitions and
" Remonstrances, so deceive his good Subjects, that
" they would pass over the Reproaches, Threats, and
" Menaces they were stuffed with; which surely
" could not be more gently reprehended by his Ma-
" jesty, than by saying, their Expressions were dif-
" ferent from the usual Language to Princes; which
" that Declaration told him, he had no occasion to
" say: But he believed, whosoever looked over that
" Declaration, presented to him at *New-market*, to
" which his was an Answer, would find the Lan-
" guage throughout it to be so Unusual, that, before
" this Parliament, it could never be paralleled; whilst,
" under pretence of justifying their Fears, they gave
" so much countenance to the discourse of the Rebels
" of *Ireland*, as if they had a mind his good Subjects
" should give credit to it: Otherwise, being warrant-
" ed by the same evidence, which they have since
" published, they would have as well declared, That
" those Rebels publicly threaten the rooting out the

BOOK
V.
"Name of the English, and that they will have a
"King of their own, and no longer be governed by
"his Majesty, as that they say, That they do no-
"thing, but by his Majesty's Authority; and that
"they call themselves the Queen's Army. And there-
"fore he had great reason to complain of the absence
"of Justice and Integrity in that Declaration; besides
"the unfitness of other Expressions.

"Neither did his Majesty mistake the Substance, or
"Logic of their Message to him, at *Theobuld's*, con-
"cerning the Militia; which was no other, and was
"stated to be no other, even by that Declaration that
"reproved him, than a plain Threat, That if his Ma-
"jesty refused to join with them, they would make a
"Law without him: Nor had the Practice since that
"time been other; which would never be justified to
"the most ordinary if not partial understandings, by
"the mere averring it to be according to the Funda-
"mental Laws of this Kingdom, without giving any
"directions, that the most Cunning and Learned
"Men in the Laws, might be able to find those Foun-
"dations And he would appeal unto all the world,
"whether they might not, with as much Justice,
"and by as much Law, have seized upon the Estate
"of every Member of both Houses, who dissented
"from that pretended Ordinance (which much the
"Major part of the House of Peers did, two or three
"several times) as they had invaded that Power of
"His over the Militia, because he, upon reasons they
"had not so much as pretended to Answer, refused
"to Consent to that Proposition.

"And if no better Effects, than loss of Time, and

"hinderance of the public Affairs, had been found
"by his Answers and Replies, all good Men might
"judge by whose Default, and whose want of Duty,
"such Effects had been; for as his End, indeed his
"only End, in those Answers and Replies, had been
"the settlement and composure of public Affairs; so,
"he was assured, and most Men did believe, that if
"that due regard and reverence had been given to his
"Words, and that consent and obedience to his
"Counsels, which he expected, there had been, be-
"fore that time, a cheerful calm upon the face of the
"whole Kingdom; every Man enjoying his own,
"with all possible peace and security that can be ima-
"gined; which surely those Men did not desire, who
"(after all those Acts of Justice, and Favor passed by
"him, this Parliament; all those Sufferings, and
"Affronts, endured and undergone by him) thought
"fit still to reproach him with Ship-money, Coat and
"Conduct-money, and other things so abundantly
"declared, as that Declaration itself confessed, in the
"general Remonstrance of the State of the Kingdom,
"published in *November* last; which his Majesty
"wondered to find now avowed to be the Remon-
"strance of both Houses; and which, he was sure,
"was presented to him only by the House of Com-
"mons; and did never, and, he was confident, in that
"time could never, have passed the House of Peers;
"the Concurrence, and Authority of which, was not
"then thought necessary. Should his Majesty believe
"those Reproaches to be the Voice of the Kingdom
"of *England*, That all his loving Subjects eased re-
"freshed, strengthened, and abundantly satisfied with

"his Acts of Grace and Favor towards them, were willing to be involved in those unthankful Expressions? He would appeal to the Thanks and Acknowledgments published in the Petitions of most of the Counties of *England*; to the Testimony, and Thanks, he had received from both Houses of Parliament; how seasonable, how agreeable that usage was to his Majesty's Merit, or their former Expressions.

"His Majesty said, he had not at all swerved, or departed from his Resolutions, or Words, in the beginning of this Parliament: He had said, he was resolved to put himself freely, and clearly upon the Love and Affection of his English Subjects; and he said so still, as far as concerns *England*. And he called Almighty God to Witness, all his Complaints and Jealousies, which had never been causeless, nor of his Houses of Parliament (but of some few Schismatical, Factious, and Ambitious Spirits; and upon grounds, as he feared, a short time would justify to the world) his Denial of the Militia, his absenting himself from *London*, had been the effects of an upright, and faithful Affection to his English Subjects; that he might be able, through all the Inconveniences he might be compelled to wrestle with, at last to preserve, and restore their Religion, Laws, and Liberties unto them.

"Since the Proceeding against the Lord *Kimbolton*, and the five Members, was still looked upon and so often pressed, as so great an advantage against his Majesty, that no Retractation made by him, nor no Action, since that time committed against Him,

" and the Law of the Land, under the pretence of
" Vindication of Privilege, could satisfy the Con-
" trivers of that Declaration, but that they would
" have his good Subjects to believe, the Accusation
" of those six Members must be a Plot for the break-
" ing the Neck of the Parliament (a strange Arro-
" gance if any of those Members had the Penning of
" that Declaration) and that it was so often urged
" against him, as if by that single, casual Mistake of
" his, in Form only, he had forfeited all Duty, Cre-
" dit, and Allegiance from his People, he said, he
" would, without endeavouring to excuse that,
" which in truth was an Error (his going to the House
" of Commons) give his People, a full, and clear
" narration of the matter of Fact; assuring himself,
" that his good Subjects would not find his carriage
" in that business, such as had been reported.

" His Majesty said, that when he resolved, upon
" such grounds, as, when they should be published,
" would satisfy the World, that it was fit for his own
" Safety, and Honor, and the Peace of the Kingdom,
" to proceed against those Persons, though he well
" knew, there was no degree of Privilege in that
" Case; yet, to show his desire of Correspondence
" with the two Houses of Parliament, he chose rather
" than to apprehend their Persons by the ordinary
" Ministers of Justice (which, according to the opi-
" nion, and practice of former times, he might have
" done) to Command his Attorney General, to ac-
" quaint his House of Peers with his intention, and
" the general matters of his Charge (which was yet
" more particular, than a mere accusation) and to

BOOK V.

"proceed accordingly; and at the same time sent a
"sworn Servant, a Serjeant at Arms, to the House of
"Commons, to acquaint them, that his Majesty did
"accuse, and intended to prosecute the five Mem-
"bers of that House for High-Treason; and did
"require, that their Persons might be secured in
"Custody. This he did, not only to show that he
"intended not to Violate, or Invade their Privileges,
"but to use more Ceremony towards them, than he
"then conceived in justice might be required of him;
"and expected at least such an Answer, as might
"inform him, if he were out of the way; but he
"received none at all; only, in the instant, without
"offering any thing of their Privileges to his con-
"sideration, an Order was made, and the same Night
"published in Print, That if any Person whatsoever,
"should offer to Arrest the Person of any Member of
"that House, without first acquainting that House
"therewith, and receiving further Order from that
"House, that it should be Lawful for such Member,
"or any Person, to resist them, and to stand upon
"his, or their Guard of Defence; and to make Re-
"sistance, according to the Protestation taken to
"Defend the Privilege of Parliament: And this was
"the first time that he heard the Protestation might
"be wrested to such a sense, or that in any Case,
"though of the most undoubted and unquestionable
"Privilege, it might be Lawful for any Person to
"resist, and use violence against a public Minister
"of Justice, armed with Lawful Authority; though
"his Majesty well knew, that even such a Minister
"might be punished for executing such Authority.

OF THE REBELLION.

"Upon Viewing that Order, his Majesty confessed, he was somewhat amazed, having never seen, or heard of the like; though he had known Members of either House committed, without so much Formality as he had used, and upon Crimes of a far inferior nature to those he had suggested; and having no course proposed him for his Proceeding, he was, upon the matter, only told, that against those Persons he was not to proceed at all; that they were above His reach, or the reach of the Law. It was not easy for him to resolve what to do: If he employed his Ministers of Justice in the usual way for their apprehension, who without doubt would not have refused to have executed his Lawful Commands, he saw what opposition, and resistance, was like to be made; which, very probably, might have cost some Blood: If he sat still, and desisted upon that Terror, he should, at the best, have confessed his own want of Power, and the weakness of the Law. In that strait, he put on a sudden Resolution, to try whether his own Presence, and a clear discovery of his Intention, which happily might not have been so well understood, could remove those Doubts, and prevent those Inconveniences, which seemed to have been threatened; and thereupon, he Resolved to go, in his own Person, to the House of Commons; which he discovered not, till the very minute of his going; when he sent out Orders, that his Servants, and such Gentlemen as were then in his Court, should attend him to *Westminster*; but giving them express Command, as he had expressed in his Answer to the Ordinance, "that no Accidents, or Provocation, should draw them to any such Action, as might imply a purpose of Force in his Majesty; And Himself, requiring those of his Train not to come within the Door, went into the House of Commons; the bare doing of which, he did not then conceive, would have been thought more a breach of Privilege, than if he had gone to the House of Peers, and sent for them to come to him; which was the usual Custom.

"He used the best Expressions he could, to assure them how far he was from any intention of violating their Privileges; that he intended to proceed legally, and speedily against the Persons he had accused; and desired therefore, if they were in the House, that they might be delivered to him; or if absent, that such course might be taken for their forth-coming, as might satisfy his just Demands; and so he departed, having no other purpose of Force, if they had been in the House, than he had before protested, before God, in his Answer to the Ordinance. They had an account now of His part of that story fully; his People might judge freely of it. What followed on Their part (though that Declaration said, it could not withdraw any part of their Reverence and Obedience from his Majesty; it might be any part of Theirs it did not) he should have too much cause hereafter to inform the World.

"His Majesty said, there would be no end of this discourse, and of upbraiding him with evil Counsellors, if, upon his constant denial of knowing any,

"they would not vouchsafe to inform him of them;
"and after eight Months amusing the Kingdom with
"the expectation of the discovery of a Malignant
"Party, and of evil Counsellors, they would not at
"last name any, nor describe them. Let the Actions
"or Lives of Men be examined, Who had Contri-
"ved, Counselled, actually consented to Grieve, and
"Burden his People; and if such were now about
"his Majesty, or any against whom any notorious,
"malicious Crime could be proved, if he sheltered
"and protected any such, let his Injustice be pub-
"lished to the World: but till that were done Parti-
"cularly and Manifestly (for he should never con-
"clude any Man upon a bare, general Vote of the
"Major part of either, or both Houses, till it were
"evident, that that Major part was without Passion
"or Affection) he must look upon the charge that
"Declaration put upon him, of cherishing and coun-
"tenancing a Discontented Party of the Kingdom
"against them, as a heavier and unjuster Tax upon
"his Justice and Honor, than any He had, or could
"lay, upon the Framers of that Declaration. And
"now, to countenance those unhandsome Expres-
"sions, whereby they usually had implied his Ma-
"jesty's Counivance at, or want of Zeal against, the
"Rebellion of *Ireland* (so odious to all good Men)
"they had found a new way of exprobration: That
"the Proclamation against those bloody Traytors
"came not out, till the beginning of *January*,
"though that Rebellion broke out in *October*, and
"then, by special Command from his Majesty, but
"forty Copies were appointed to be Printed. His

BOOK V.

"Majesty said it was well known where he was at that time, when that Rebellion broke forth; in *Scotland*: That He immediately, from thence, recommended the Care of that Business to both Houses of Parliament here, after he had provided for all fitting Supplies from his Kingdom of *Scotland*: That after his return hither, he observed all those Forms for that Service, which he was advised to by his Council of *Ireland*, or both Houses of Parliament here, and if no Proclamation issued out sooner (of which, for the present, he was not certain; but thought that others, by his directions, were issued before that time) it was, because the Lords Justices of the Kingdom desired them no sooner; and when they did, the Number they desired was but Twenty; which they advised might be signed by his Majesty; which he, for expedition of the Service, commanded to be Printed, a Circumstance not required by them; thereupon he signed more of them, than his Justices desired; all which was very well known to some Members of one, or both Houses of Parliament; who had the more to Answer, if they forbore to express it at the passing of that Declaration; and if they did express it, he had the greater reason to complain, that so envious an Aspersion should be cast on his Majesty to his People, when they knew well how to Answer their own Objection.

"What that Complaint was against the Parliament, put forth in His Name, which was such an Evidence and Countenance to the Rebels, and spoke the same Language of the Parliament which the Rebels did; he said he could not understand.

"All his Answers and Declarations had been, and were, owned by himself; and had been attested under his own hand, if any other had been published in his Name, and without his Authority, it would be easy for both Houses of Parliament to discover, and apprehend the Authors: And he wished, that whosoever was trusted with the Drawing, and Penning that Declaration, had no more Authority, or Cunning to impose upon, or deceive a Major part of those Votes, by which it passed, than any Man had to prevail with his Majesty to publish in his Name any thing, but the sense, and Resolution of his own Heart; or that the Contriver of that Declaration could, with as good a Conscience, call God to witness, that all his Counsels and Endeavours had been free from all private Aims, personal Respects or Passions whatsoever, as his Majesty had done, and did. That he never had, or knew of any such Resolution of bringing up the Army to *London*.

"And since that new Device was found out instead of Answering his reasons, or satisfying his just demands, to blast his Declarations and Answers, as if they were not his own; a bold, senseless Imputation: He said he was sure, that every Answer, and Declaration, published by his Majesty, was much more his own, than any one of those bold, threatening, and reproachful Petitions, and Remonstrances, were the Acts of either, or both Houses. And if the Penner of that Declaration had been careful of the Trust reposed in him, he would never have denied (and thereupon found fault with his Majesty's just indignation) in the

BOOK V.

"Text or Margin, that his Majesty had never been charged with the Intention of any Force; and that in their whole Declaration, there was no one word tending to any such reproach; the contrary whereof was so evident, that his Majesty was, in express terms, charged in that Declaration, that he had sent them gracious Messages, when, with His privity, bringing up the Army was in agitation; and, even in that Declaration, they sought to make the People believe some such thing to be proved, in the Depositions therewith published; wherein, his Majesty doubted not, they would as much fail, as they did in their Censure of that Petition, showed formerly to his Majesty by Captain *Leg*, and subscribed by him C. R. which, notwithstanding his Majesty's full, and particular Narration of the substance of that Petition, the circumstances of seeing and approving it, that Declaration was pleased to say, was full of Scandal to the Parliament, and might have proved dangerous to the whole Kingdom. If they had that dangerous Petition in their hands, his Majesty said, he had no reason to believe any tenderness towards Him had kept them from communicating it; if they had it not, his Majesty ought to have been believed: But that all good People might compute their other pretended dangers by their clear understanding of that, the noise whereof had not been inferior to any of the rest, his Majesty said, he had recovered a true Copy of the very Petition he had signed with C. R. which should, in fit time, be published; and which, he hoped, would open the eyes of his good People.

"Concerning his Warrant for Mr. *Jermyn*'s

"Paſſage, his Anſwer was true, and full; but for his
"black Sattin Suit, and white Boots, he could give
"no Account.

"His Majeſty had complained in his Declaration,
"and, as often as he ſhould have occaſion to mention
"his return, and reſidence near *London*, he ſhould
"complain, of the barbarous and ſeditious Tumults
"at *White-Hall*, and *Weſtminſter*; which indeed had
"been ſo full of Scandal to his Government, and
"danger to his Perſon, that he ſhould never think
"of his return thither, till he had Juſtice for what
"was paſt, and Security for the time to come: And
"if there were ſo great a neceſſity, or deſire of his
"return, as was pretended, in all this time, upon ſo
"often preſſing his deſires, and upon cauſes ſo noto-
"rious, he ſhould at leaſt have procured ſome Order
"for the future. But that Declaration told his Ma-
"jeſty he was upon the matter miſtaken; the reſort
"of the Citizens to *Weſtminſter* was as lawful, as the
"reſort of great Numbers every day in the Term to
"the Ordinary Courts of Juſtice; They knew no
"Tumults Strange! was the diſorderly appearance
"of ſo many thouſand People, with Staves and
"Swords, crying through the Streets, *Weſtminſter-
"Hall*, the Paſſage between both Houſes (inſomuch
"as the Members could hardly paſs to and fro) *No
"Biſhops, down with the Biſhops*, No Tumults?
"What Member was there of either Houſe, that
"ſaw not thoſe Numbers, and heard not thoſe Cries?
"And yet lawful Aſſemblies! Were not ſeveral
"Members of either Houſe, aſſaulted, threatened,
"and evilly treated? And yet no Tumults! Why
"made the Houſe of Peers a Declaration, and ſent it

"down to the House of Commons for the suppres-
"sing of Tumults, if there were no Tumults? And
"if there were any, why was not such a Declaration
"consented to, and published? When the Attempts
"were so visible, and threats so loud to pull down
"the Abby at *Westminster*, had not his Majesty just
"cause to apprehend, that such People might con-
"tinue their work to *White-Hall*? Yet no Tumults?
"What a strange time are We in, that a few im-
"pudent, malicious (to give them no worse term)
"Men, should cast such a Mist of error before the
"eyes of both Houses of Parliament, as that they
"either could not, or would not, see how manifestly
"they injured themselves, by maintaining those
"visible untruths. His Majesty said, he would say no
"more: by the help of God and the Law, he would
"have Justice for those Tumults.

"From excepting how weightily every Man
"might judge, to what his Majesty had said, that
"Declaration proceeded to censure him for what he
"had not said; for the prudent Omissions in his
"Answers: His Majesty had forborne to say any thing
"of the words spoken at *Kensington*; or the Articles
"against his dearest Consort, and the Accusation of
"the six Members: Of the last, his Majesty said, he
"had spoken often; and he thought, enough of
"the other two; but having never accused any
"(though God knew what truth there might be in
"either) he had no reason to give any particular
"Answer.

"He said, he did not reckon himself bereaved of
"any part of his Prerogative; which he was pleased

" freely, for a time, to part with by Bill; yet he must
" say, he expressed a great Trust in his two Houses
" of Parliament, when he divested himself of the
" power of dissolving this Parliament; which was a
" just, necessary, and proper Prerogative. But he was
" glad to hear their resolution, that it should not
" encourage them to do any thing which otherwise
" had not been fit to have been done: If it did, it
" would be such a breach of Trust, as God would
" require an Account for at their hands.

" For the Militia, he said so much of it before, and
" the Point was so well understood by all Men, that
" he would waste time no more in that Dispute. He
" never had said, there was no such thing as an Or-
" dinance, though he knew that they had been long
" disused, but that there was never any Ordinance,
" or could be any, without the King's consent; and
" that was true: And the unnecessary Precedent,
" cited in that Declaration, did not offer to prove
" the contrary. But enough of that; God and the Law
" must determine that business.

" Neither had that Declaration, given his Majesty
" any satisfaction concerning the Votes of the
" fifteenth and sixteenth of *March* last; which he must
" declare, and appeal to all the world in the Point,
" to be the greatest violation of his Majesty's Privi-
" lege, the Law of the Land, the Liberty of the
" Subject, and the Right of Parliament, that could
" be imagined. One of those Votes was, and there
" would need no other to destroy the King and
" People. That when the Lords and Commons (it is
" well the Commons are admitted to their part in

"Judicature) shall declare what the Law of the Land is, the same must be assented to and obeyed; that is the sense in few words. Where is every Man's Property; every Man's Liberty? If the Major part of both Houses declare, that the Law is that the younger Brother shall inherit; what is become of all the Families, and Estates in the Kingdom? If they declare, that by the Fundamental Laws of the Land, such a rash Action, such an unadvised Word, ought to be punished by perpetual Imprisonment, is not the Liberty of the Subject, *durante beneplacito*, remediless? That Declaration confesses, they pretend not to a power of making new Laws; that without his Majesty, they could not do That: They need no such power, if their Declaration could suspend this Statute from being obeyed, or executed. If they had power to declare the Lord *Digby's* waiting upon his Majesty, at *Hampton-Court*, and thence visiting some Officers at *Kingston*, with a Coach and six Horses, to be levying of War, and High-Treason; and Sir *John Hotham's* defying his Majesty to his face, keeping his Majesty's Town, Fort, and Goods against him, by force of Arms, to be an Act of Affection, and Loyalty; What needed a power of making new Laws? Or would there be such a thing as Law left?

"He desired his good Subjects to mark the reason, and consequence of those Votes; the progress they had already made, and how infinite the progress might be. First, they Voted the Kingdom was in Imminent danger (it was now above three Months since they discerned it) from Enemies abroad, and

from

"from a Popish, and disaffected party at home; that
"is matter of Fact; the Law follows: This Vote had
"given them Authority by Law, the Fundamental
"Laws of the Kingdom, to order and dispose of the
"Militia of the Kingdom; and, with this Power, and
"to prevent that danger, to enter into his Majesty's
"Towns, seize upon his Magazine, and, by Force,
"keep both from him. Was not that his Majesty's
"Case? First, they Vote he had an Intention to levy
"War against his Parliament; that is matter of Fact;
"Then they declare such as shall assist him, to be
"guilty of High-Treason; that is the Law, and
"proved by two Statutes, Themselves knew to be
"repealed. No matter for that, They declare it.
"Upon this ground they exercise the Militia; and so
"actually do that upon his Majesty, which they had
"Voted He intended to do upon Them. Who could
"not see the confusion, that must follow upon such
"Power of Declaring? If they should now Vote that
"his Majesty did not write this Declaration, but that
"such a One did it, which was still matter of Fact;
"and then Declare, that for so doing, he was an
"Enemy to the Common-wealth; what was become
"of the Law that man was born to? And if all their
"Zeal for the defence of the Law, were but to defend
"that which They Declared to be Law; their own
"Votes; it would not be in their power to satisfy any
"Man of their good Intentions to the public Peace,
"but such who were willing to relinquish their Title
"to *Magna Charta*, and hold their Lives, and For-
"tunes, by a Vote of the Major part of both Houses.
"In a word, his Majesty denied not, but they

"might have power to declare in a particular, doubt-
"ful Case, regularly brought before them, what
"Law is: But to make a general Declaration,
"whereby the known rule of the Law might be
"crossed, or altered, they had no power; nor could
"exercise any, without bringing the Life and
"Liberty of the Subject to a Lawless, and Arbitrary
"Subjection.

"His Majesty had complained (and the world
"might Judge of the Justice, and Necessity of that
"complaint) of the multitude of seditious Pamphlets,
"and Sermons; and that Declaration told him, they
"knew he had ways enough in his ordinary Courts
"of Justice to punish those; so his Majesty said, he
"had to punish Tumults and Riots; and yet they
"would not serve his turn to keep his Towns, his
"Forests, and Parks from violence. And it might
"be, though those Courts had still the Power to
"punish, they might have lost the skill to define,
"what Tumults and Riots are; otherwise a Jury in
"*Southwark*, legally impannelled to examine a Riot
"there, would not have been superseded and the
"Sheriff injoined not to proceed, by virtue of an
"Order of the House of Commons; which, it seemed,
"at that time had the sole power of Declaring. But it
"was no wonder that they who could not see the
"Tumults, did not consider the Pamphlets and
"Sermons; though the Author of the *Protestation*
"*Protested*, were well known to be *Burton* (that in-
"famous disturber of the Peace of the Church and
"State) and that he Preached it at *Westminster*, in the
"bearing of divers Members of the House of Com-

" mons. But of such Pamphlets and seditious Preachers (divers whereof had been recommended, if not imposed upon several Parishes, by some Members of both Houses, by what Authority his Majesty knew not)he would hereafter take a furtherAccount.

" His Majesty said, he confessed he had little skill in the Laws; and those that had had most, he found now were much to seek: Yet he could not understand or believe, that every ordinary Court, or any Court, had power to raise what Guard they pleased, and under what Command they pleased, Neither could he imagine what dangerous Effects they found by the Guard he appointed them; or indeed any the least occasion, why they needed any Guard at all.

" But of all the Imputations, so causelesly and unjustly laid upon his Majesty by that Declaration, he said, he must wonder at that Charge so apparently, and evidently Untrue; That such were continually preferred and countenanced by him, who were friends or favorers or related unto the chief Authors, and Actors of that Arbitrary Power heretofore practised, and complained of: And on the other side, that such as did appear against it, were daily discountenanced, and disgraced. He said, he would know One Person that contributed to the ills of those times, or had depandance upon those that did, whom he did or lately had countenanced, or preferred; nay he was confident (and he looked for no other at their hands) as they had been always most Eminent Asserters of the public Liberties; so if they found his Majesty inclined to any thing not agreeable to Honor and Justice, they would leave "him to morrow. Whether different Persons had not, and did not receive countenance elsewhere, and upon what grounds, all men might judge; and whether his Majesty had not been forward enough to honor and prefer those of the most contrary opinion, how little comfort soever he had of those Preferments, in bestowing of which, hereafter, he would be more guided by Men's Actions, than Opinions. And therefore he had good cause to bestow that admonition (for his Majesty assured them, it was an admonition of his Own) upon both his Houses of Parliament, to take heed of inclining, under the specious shows of Necessity and Danger, to the exercise of such an Arbitrary Power, they before complained of: the Advice would do no harm, and he should be glad to see it followed.

" His Majesty asked, if all specious Promises, and loud Professions, of making him a great and glorious King; of settling a greater Revenue upon his Majesty, than any of his Ancestors had enjoyed; of making him to be honored at home, and feared abroad; were resolved into this, That they would be ready to settle his Revenue in an Honorable proportion, when he should put himself in such a posture of Government, that his Subjects might be secure to enjoy his just Protection for their Religion, Laws, and Liberties? What posture of Government they intended, he knew not; nor could he imagine what security his good Subjects could desire for their Religion, Laws, and Liberties, which he had not offered or fully given. And was it suitable to the Duty, and Dignity of both Houses of Parliament, to Answer his particular, weighty

"Expressions of the causes of his remove from *Lon-*
"*don*, so generally known to the Kingdom, with
"a Scoff; That they hoped he was driven from
"thence, not by his own fears, but by the fears of
"the Lord *Digby*, and his retinue of Cavaliers? Sure,
"his Majesty said, the Penner of that Declaration,
"inserted that ungrave and insolent Expression, as
"he had done divers others, without the consent,
"or examination of both Houses; who would not
"so lightly have departed from their former pro-
"fessions of Duty to his Majesty.

"Whether the way to a good understanding be-
"tween his Majesty, and his People, had been as
"zealously pressed by Them, as it had been professed,
"and desired by Him, would be easily discerned
"by them who observed that He had left no public
"Act undone on His part, which, in the least de-
"gree, might be necessary to the peace, plenty,
"and security of his Subjects: And that They had
"not dispatched one Act, which had given the least
"evidence of their particular affection, and kindness
"to his Majesty; but on the contrary, had discoun-
"tenanced and hindered the Testimony other Men
"would give to him of their affections. Witness the
"stopping, and keeping back the Bill of Subsidies,
"granted by the Clergy almost a year since; which,
"though his Personal wants were so notoriously
"known, they would not, to that time, pass; so not
"only forbearing to supply his Majesty themselves,
"but keeping the love and bounty of other Men
"from him; and affording no other Answers to all his
"desires, all his reasons (indeed not to be Answered)

BOOK V.

"than that he muſt not make his underſtanding, or
"reaſon, the Rule of his Government; but ſuffer
"himſelf to be aſſiſted (which his Majeſty never
"denied) by his Great Council. He ſaid, he required
"no other Liberty to his Will, than the meaneſt of
"Them did (he wiſhed they would always uſe that
"Liberty) not to conſent to any thing evidently
"contrary to his conſcience, and underſtanding:
"And he had, and ſhould always give as much eſti-
"mation, and regard to the Advice, and Counſel of
"both Houſes of Parliament, as ever Prince had
"done: But he ſhould never, and he hoped his Peo-
"ple would never, account the Contrivance of a
"few Factious, Seditious Perſons. a Malignant Party,
"who would ſacrifice the Common-wealth to their
"own fury and ambition, the Wiſdom of Parliament;
"and that the juſtifying, and defending of ſuch Per-
"ſons (of whom, and of their particular, ſiniſter
"ways, to compaſs their own bad ends, his Majeſty
"would ſhortly inform the world) was not the way
"to preſerve Parliaments, but was the oppoſing, and
"preferring a few unworthy Perſons, before their
"Duty to their King, or their Care of the Kingdom.
"They would have his Majeſty remember, that His
"Reſolutions did concern Kingdoms, and therefore
"were not to be moulded by his own underſtanding:
"He ſaid, he did well remember it; but he would have
"Them remember, that when their Conſultations
"endeavoured to leſſen the Office, and Dignity of a
"King, they meddled with that which is not within
"their determination, and of Which his Majeſty muſt
"give an account to God, and his other Kingdoms,
"and muſt maintain with the Sacrifice of his Life.

" Laſtly, that Declaration told the People of a present, deſperate, and malicious Plot the Malignant Party was then acting, under the plauſible notions of ſtirring Men up to a care of preſerving the King's Prerogative; maintaining the diſcipline of the Church, upholding and continuing the reverence, and ſolemnity of God's Service; and encouraging Learning (indeed plauſible, and Honorable notions to act any thing upon) and that upon thoſe grounds divers mutinous Petitions had been framed in *London*, *Kent*, and other places: His Majeſty aſked upon what grounds theſe Men would have Petitions framed? Had ſo many Petitions, even againſt the form, and conſtitution of the Kingdom and the Laws eſtabliſhed, been joyfully received, and accepted? And ſhould Petitions framed upon thoſe grounds be called Mutinous? Had a multitude of mean, unknown, inconſiderable, contemptible Perſons, about the City, and Suburbs of *London*, had liberty to Petition againſt the Government of the Church, againſt the Book of Common-Prayer, againſt the Freedom, and Privilege of Parliament, and been thanked for it: and ſhould it be called Mutiny, in the greateſt and beſt Citizens of *London*, and the Gentry and Commonalty of *Kent*, to frame Petitions upon thoſe grounds; and to deſire to be governed by the known Laws of the Land, not by Orders and Votes of either, or both Houſes? Could this be thought the Wiſdom, and Juſtice of both Houſes of Parliament? Was it not evidently the work of a Faction, within or without both Houſes, who deceived the Truſt repoſed in

" them; and had now told his Majesty, what Mutiny
" was? To stir Men up to a care of preserving his
" Prerogative, maintaining the discipline of the
" Church, upholding and continuing the reverence,
" and solemnity of God's Service, encouraging of
" Learning, was Mutiny. Let Heaven and Earth,
" God and Man, judge between his Majesty and
" these Men: And however such Petitions were there
" called Mutinous; and the Petitioners threatened,
" discountenanced, censured, and imprisoned; if
" they brought such Petitions to his Majesty he
" would graciously receive them; and defend Them
" and their Rights, against what Power soever, with
" the utmost hazard of his being.

" His Majesty said, he had been the longer, to his
" very great pain, in this Answer, that he might give
" the world satisfaction, even in the most trivial Par-
" ticulars, which had been objected against him;
" and that he might not be again reproached, with
" any more prudent Omissions. If he had been com-
" pelled to sharper Language, than his Majesty affect-
" ed, it might be considered, how vile, how insuf-
" ferable his Provocations had been: And, except
" to repel force were to assault, and to give punctual
" and necessary Answers to rough and insolent De-
" mands, were to make Invectives, he was confident
" the world would accuse his Majesty of too much
" mildness; and all his good Subjects would think,
" he was not well dealt with; and would judge of
" his Majesty, and of their own happiness, and secu-
" rity in him, by his Actions; which he desired might
" no longer prosper, or have a Blessing from God

"upon them, and his Majesty, than they should be
"directed to the Glory of God in the maintenance of
"the true Protestant Profession; to the preservation
"of the Property and Liberty of the Subject, in the
"observation of the Laws; and to the maintenance
"of the Rights and Freedom of Parliament, in the al-
"lowance and protection of all their just Privileges."

This Declaration was no sooner published, but his Majesty likewise set forth an Answer to that other Declaration, of the 26th of *May*; in which he said, "That whosoever looked over the late Remon-
"strance, Entitled *A Declaration of the Lords and*
"*Commons, of the 26th of May*, would not think that
"his Majesty had great reason to be pleased with it;
"yet he could not but commend the plain dealing,
"and ingenuity of the framers, and contrivers of that
"Declaration (which had been wrought in a hotter
"and quicker Forge than any of the rest) who would
"no longer suffer his Majesty to be Affronted by
"being told, They would make him a great and glo-
"rious King; whilst they used all possible skill, to
"reduce him to extreme want, and indigency; and
"that they would make him to be loved at Home,
"and feared Abroad; whilst they endeavoured, by
"all possible ways, to render him odious to his good
"Subjects, and contemptible to all Foreign Princes;
"but, like round dealing Men, told him, in plain
"English, That they had done him no wrong, because
"he was not capable of receiving any; and that they
"had taken nothing from him, because he had
"never any thing of his own to lose. If that Doctrine
"were true, and that indeed he ought to be of no

BOOK V.

The King's Answer to the Declaration of May 26, 1642.

"other confideration, than they had informed his
"People in that Declaration, that Gentleman was
"much more excufable, that faid publicly, unre-
"proved, That the happinefs of the Kingdom did
"not depend on his Majefty, or upon any of the
"Royal branches of that Root: And the other, who
"faid, his Majefty was not worthy to be King of
"*England*: Language very monftrous to be allowed
"by either Houfe of Parliament; and of which, by
"the help of God, and the Law, he muft have fome
"Examination. But, he doubted not, all his good
"Subjects did now plainly difcern, through the maf-
"que and vizard of their Hypocrify, what their
"defign was; and would no more look upon the Fra-
"mers and Contrivers of that Declaration, as upon
"both Houfes of Parliament (whofe Freedom, and
"juft Privileges he would always maintain; and in
"whofe behalf, he was as much fcandalized as for
"Himfelf) but as a Faction of Malignant, and Schif-
"matical, and Ambitious Perfons; whofe defign was,
"and always had been, to alter the whole frame of
"Government, both of Church and State; and to
"fubject both King and People to their own Lawlefs,
"Arbitrary Power, and Government: of whofe
"Perfons, and of whofe defigns, his Majefty faid,
"he would, within a very fhort time, give his good
"Subjects and the World a full, and, he hoped, a
"fatisfactory Narration.

"The Contrivers and Penners of that Declaration
"(of whom his Majefty would be only underftood
"to fpeak, when he mentioned any of their undutiful
"Acts againft him) faid, that the great Affairs of the

"Kingdom, and the miserable bleeding Condition of
" Ireland, would afford them little leisure to spend
" their time in Declarations, Answers, and Replies.
" Indeed, his Majesty said, the miserable, and deplor-
" able Condition of both Kingdoms, would require
" somewhat else at their hands: But he would gladly
" know how they had spent their time since the
" recess (then almost eight Months) but in Declara-
" tions, Remonstrances, and Invectives against his
" Majesty, and his Government; or in preparing
" matter for them. Had his Majesty invited them to
" any such expense of time, by beginning Arguments
" of that Nature? Their Leisure, or their Inclination,
" was not as they pretended: And what was their
" printing and publishing their Petitions to him; their
" Declarations, and Remonstrances of him; their
" odious Votes and Resolutions, sometimes of one,
" sometimes of both Houses, against his Majesty
" (never in that manner communicated before this
" Parliament) but an Appeal to the People? And,
" in God's name, let them judge of the Persons they
" had trusted.

" Their first quarrel was (as it was always, to let
" them into their frank expressions of his Majesty,
" and his Actions) against the Malignant Party;
" whom they were pleased still to call, and never to
" prove to be his evil Counsellors. But indeed nothing
" was more evident by their whole Proceedings,
" than that by the Malignant Party, they intended
" all the Members of both Houses who agreed not
" with them in their Opinion (thence had come their
" distinction of good, and bad Lords; of Persons ill

"affected to the House of Commons; who had been "proscribed, and their Names listed, and read in Tu-"mults) and all the Persons of the Kingdom who ap-"prove not of their Actions. So that, if in truth they "would be ingenuous, and name the Persons they "intended; Who would be the Men, upon whom "the imputation of Malignity would be cast, but "They who had stood stoutly, and immutably for "the Religion, the Liberties, the Laws, for all public "Interest? (so long as there was any to be stood for) "They, who had always been, and still were, as "zealous Professors, and some of them as able, and "earnest Defenders of the Protestant Doctrine against "the Church of *Rome*, as any were; Who had often, "and earnestly besought his Majesty to consent, that "no indifferent, and unnecessary Ceremony, might "be pressed upon weak, and tender consciences, "and that he would agree to a Bill for that purpose? "They to whose Wisdom, Courage, and Counsel, "the Kingdom owed as much as it could to Subjects; "and upon whose unblemished Lives, Envy itself "could lay no imputation; nor endeavoured to lay "any, until their Virtues brought them to his Ma-"jesty's Knowledge, and Favor? His Majesty said, if "the Contrivers of that Declaration would be faith-"ful to themselves, and consider all those Persons of "both Houses, whom they, in their own consciences, "knew to dissent from them in the Matter, and Lan-"guage of that Declaration, and in all those unduti-"ful Actions of which he complained, they would "be found in Honor, Fortune, Wisdom, Reputation, "and Weight, if not in Number, much superior to "them. So much for the evil Counsellors.

" Then what was the evil Counsel itself? His Ma-
" jesty's coming from *London* (where He, and many,
" whose affections to him were very eminent, were
" in danger every day to be torn in pieces) to *York*;
" where his Majesty, and all such as would put them-
" selves under his Protection, might live, he thanked
" God and the Loyalty and Affection of that good
" People, very securely: His not submitting himself
" absolutely (and renouncing his own understand-
" ing) to the Votes, and Resolutions of the Contri-
" vers of that Declaration, when they told his Ma-
" jesty, that they were above him; and might, by his
" own Authority, do with his Majesty what they
" pleased: and his not being contented, that all his
" good Subjects, Lives, and Fortunes, should be dis-
" posed of by their Votes; but by the known Law
" of the Land. This was the evil Counsel given, and
" taken: And would not all Men believe, there
" needed much power and skill of the Malignant
" Party, to infuse that Counsel into him? And then,
" to apply the Argument the Contrivers of that De-
" claration made for themselves, was it probable or
" possible, that such Men, whom his Majesty had
" mentioned (who must have so great a share in the
" misery) should take such pains in the procuring
" thereof; and spend so much time, and run so many
" hazards, to make themselves Slaves, and to ruin
" the Freedom of this Nation?

" His Majesty said (with a clear, and upright Con-
" science to God Almighty) whosoever harboured
" the least thought in his breast, of ruining or violat-
" ing the public Liberty, or Religion of the Kingdom,

"or the just Freedom and Privilege of Parliament,
"let him be Accursed; and he should be no Coun-
"sellor of His, that would not say *Amen.* For the
"Contrivers of that Declaration, he had not said
"any thing, which might imply any Inclination in
"them to be Slaves. That which he had charged
"them with, was invading the public Liberty; and
"his presumption might be very strong and vehe-
"ment, that, though they had no mind to be Slaves,
"they were not unwilling to be Tyrants: What is
"Tyranny, but to admit no rules to govern by, but
"their own Wills? And they knew the misery of
"*Athens* was at the highest, when it suffered under
"the thirty Tyrants.

"His Majesty said, if that Declaration had told
"him (as indeed it might, and as in justice it ought
"to have done) that the Precedents of any of his
"Ancestors did fall short, and much below what had
"been done by Him, this Parliament, in point of
"Grace, and Favor to his People; he should not
"otherwise have wondered at it, than at such a truth
"in such a place. But when to justify their having
"done more than ever their Predecessors did, it told
"his good Subjects (as most injuriously and inso-
"lently it did) that the highest, and most unwarrant-
"able Precedents of any of his Predecessors did fall
"short, and much below what had been done to
"them this Parliament by Him, he must confess him-
"self amazed, and not able to understand them; and
"he must tell those ungrateful Men (who durst tell
"their King, that they might, without want of Mo-
"desty and Duty, Depose him) that the condition of
"his Subjects, when, by whatsoever Accidents and

"Conjunctures of time, it was at worst under his
"power, unto which, by no default of His, they
"should be ever again reduced, was, by many de-
"grees, more pleasant and happy, than that to which
"their furious pretence of Reformation had brought
"them. Neither was his Majesty affraid of the high-
"est Precedents of other Parliaments; which those
"men Boldly (his good Subjects would call it worse)
"told him they might, without want of Modesty or
"Duty, make their Patterns. If he had no other se-
"curity against those Precedents, but Their modesty
"and duty, he was in a miserable condition, as all
"Persons would be who depended upon Them.

"That Declaration would not allow his Inference,
"that by avowing the Act of Sir *John Hotham*, they
"did destroy the Title, and Interest of all his Sub-
"jects to their Lands, and Goods; but confessed, if
"they were found Guilty of that Charge, it were
"indeed a very great Crime. And did they not, in
"that Declaration, admit themselves guilty of that
"very Crime? Did they not say, Who doubts but
"that a Parliament may dispose of any thing, wherein
"his Majesty, or his Subjects had a right, in such a
"way as that the Kingdom might not be in danger
"thereby? Did they not then call Themselves this
"Parliament, and challenge that Power without his
"Consent? Did they not extend that Power to all
"Cases, where, the necessity or Common Good of
"the Kingdom was concerned? And did they not
"arrogate to themselves alone, the Judgment of
"that Danger, that Necessity, and that Common
"Good of the Kingdom? What was, if that were

"not, to unsettle the security of all Men's Estates;
"and to expose them to an Arbitrary Power of their
"own? If a Faction should at any time by cunning,
"or force, or absence, or accident, prevail over a
"Major part of both Houses; and pretend that there
"were evil Counsellors, a Malignant Party, about
"the King; by whom the Religion, and Liberty of
"the Kingdom, were both in danger (this they
"might do, they had done it then) they might take
"away, be it from the King, or People, whatsoever
"they, in their judgments, should think fit. This
"was Lawful, they had declared it so: Let the
"world judge, whether his Majesty had charged
"them unjustly: and whether they were not guilty
"of the Crime, which themselves confessed (being
"proved) was a great One; and how safely his Ma-
"jesty might commit the power, those People de-
"sired, into Their hands; who, in all probability,
"would be no sooner possessed of it, than they
"would revive that Tragedy, which Mr. *Hooker*
"related of the Anabaptists in *Germany*; who, talk-
"ing of nothing but Faith, and of the true Fear of
"God, and that Riches and Honor were Vanity; at
"first, upon the great opinion of their Humility,
"Zeal, and Devotion, procured much reverence,
"and estimation with the People; after finding how
"many Persons they had ensnared with their Hypo-
"crisy, they begun to propose to themselves to re-
"form both the Ecclesiastical, and Civil Govern-
"ment of the State: Then, because possibly they
"might meet with some opposition, they secretly
"entered into a League of Association; and shortly

after,

" after, finding the power they had gotten with the
" credulous People, enriched themselves with all
" kind of Spoil and Pillage; and justified them-
" selves upon our Saviour's promise, *The meek shall
inherit the Earth*; and declared Their Title was the
" same which the righteous *Israelites* had to the
" Goods of the wicked *Egyptians*: His Majesty said,
" this story was worth the reading at large, and nee-
" ded no application.

" But his Majesty might by no means say, that He
" had the same Title to his Town of *Hull*, and the
" Ammunition there, as any of his Subjects had to
" their Land, or Money: That was a Principle,
" that pulled up the Foundation of the Liberty and
" Property of every Subject. Why? because the
" King's Property in his Towns, and in his Goods
" bought with the public Money, as they conceive
" his Magazine at *Hull* to be, was inconsistent with
" the Subjects' property in their Lands, Goods, and
" Liberty. Did those Men think, that as they assu-
" med a power of declaring Law (and whatsoever
" contradicted that Declaration broke their Privi-
" leges) so that they had a power of declaring Sense,
" and Reason, and imposing Logic, and Syllogisms
" on the Schools, as well as Law upon the People?
" Did not all Mankind know that several Men
" might have several Rights, and Interests in the self-
" same House and Land, and yet neither destroy the
" other? Was not the Interest of the Lord *Paramount*
" consistent with that of the Mesne Lord; and His
" with that of the Tenant; and yet their Properties
" or Interests not at all confounded? And why

" might not his Majesty then have a full, Lawful
" Interest, and Property in his Town of *Hull* and
" yet his Subjects have a Property in their Houses
" too? But he could not sell, or give away at his
" Pleasure this Town and Fort, as a private Man
" might do his Lands or Goods. What then? Many
" men have no Authority to let, or set their Leases,
" or sell their Land, have they therefore no Title to
" them, or Interest in them? May they be taken
" from them, because they cannot sell them? He
" said, the purpose of his Journey to *Hull*, was neither
" to sell, or give it away.

" But for the Magazine, the Munition there, that
" he bought with his own Money, he might surely
" have sold that, lent, or given it away. No; he
" bought it with the public Money, and the Proof
" is. They conceive it so; and, upon that Conceit,
" had Voted, that it should be taken from him. Ex-
" cellent Justice! suppose his Majesty had kept that
" Money by him, and not bought Arms with it,
" would they have taken it from him upon that
" Conceit: Nay might they not, wheresoever that
" Money was (for through how many hands soever
" it hath passed, it is the public Money still, if ever
" it were) seize it, and take it from the owners?
" But the Towns, Forts, Magazines, and King-
" dom, is intrusted to his Majesty; and he is a
" Person trusted. His Majesty said, he was so, God,
" and the Law had trusted him; and he had taken an
" Oath to discharge that Trust, for the good and
" safety of the People. What Oaths They had taken,
" he knew not, unless those, which, in that violence,
" they had manifestly, maliciously violated. Might

"any thing be taken from a Man, becaufe he is
"trufted with it? Nay, may the Perfon himfelf take
"away the thing he trufts, when he will, and in
"what manner he will? The Law had been other-
"wife, and, he believed, would be fo held, notwith-
"ftanding their Declarations.

"But that Truft ought to be managed by their
"Advice, and the Kingdom had trufted Them for
"that purpofe. Impoffible, that the fame Truft
"fhould be irrecoverably committed to his Majefty,
"and his Heirs for ever, and the fame Truft, and a
"Power above that Truft (for fo was the Power
"they pretended) be committed to others. Did not
"the People, that fent them, look upon them as a
"body but temporary, and diffolvable at his Ma-
"jefty's pleafure? And could it be believed, that
"they intended them for his Guardians, and Con-
"trollers in the managing of that Truft, which God
"and the Law had granted to Him, and to his
"Pofterity for ever? What the extent of the Com-
"miffion, and Truft was, nothing could better
"teach them than the Writ, whereby they are met.
"His Majefty faid, he called them (and without
"that call, they could not have come together) to
"be his Counfellors, not Commanders (for how-
"ever they frequently confounded them, the Offices
"were feveral) and Counfellors not in all things,
"but in fome things, *de quibufdam arduis*, &c. And
"they would eafily find among their Precedents,
"that Queen *Eliz.* upon whofe time all good Men
"looked with reverence, committed one *Wentworth*,
"a Member of the Houfe of Commons, to the

"Tower, sitting the House, but for proposing that
"they might advise the Queen in a matter she
"thought they had nothing to do to meddle in. But
"his Majesty is trusted: And is He the only Person
"trusted? And might they do what their own incli-
"nation and fury led them to? Were They not
"trusted by his Majesty, when he first sent for them;
"and were they not trusted by him, when he passed
"them his promise, that he would not Dissolve
"them? Could it be presumed (and presumptions
"go far with Them) that he trusted them with a
"power to destroy himself, and to dissolve his Go-
"vernment, and Authority? If the People might be
"allowed to make an equitable construction of the
"Laws and Statutes, a Doctrine avowed by them,
"would not all his good Subjects swear, he never
"intended by that Act of Continuance, that they
"should do what they have since done? Were they
"not trusted by those that sent them? And were
"they trusted to alter the Government of Church
"and State; and to make themselves perpetual Dic-
"tators over the King, and People? Did they in-
"tend, that the Law itself should be subject to their
"Votes; and that whatsoever They said, or did,
"should be Lawful, because They Declared it so?
"The Oaths they had taken who sent them, and
"without taking which, themselves were not capa-
"ble of their place in Parliament, made the one in-
"capable of giving, and the other of receiving such
"a Trust; unless they could persuade his good Sub-
"jects, that his Majesty is the only supreme Head,
"and Governor in all Causes, and over all Persons,
"within his Dominions; and yet that They had a

"Power over him to constrain him to manage his
"Trust, and Govern his Power, according to their
"Discretion.

"The Contrivers of that Declaration told his
"Majesty, that they would never allow him (an
"humble, and dutiful expression) to be judge of the
"Law; That belonged only to Them; They might,
"and must, judge and declare. His Majesty, said,
"they all knew what power the Pope, under pre-
"tence of interpreting Scriptures, and declaring Ar-
"ticles of Faith, though he decline the making the
"one or the other, had usurped over Men's consci-
"ences; and that, under color of having power of
"ordering all things for the Good of Men's Souls, he
"entitles himself to all the Kingdoms of the world:
"He would not accuse the Framers of that Declara-
"tion (how bold soever they were with his Majesty)
"that they inclined to Popery, of which another
"Maxim was, That all Men must submit their
"Reason and Understanding, and the Scripture it-
"self, to that declaring power of his: Neither would
"he tell them, though They had told Him so, that
"they use the very Language of the Rebels of *Ire-*
"*land*: and yet they say those Rebels declare, that
"whatsoever they do, is for the Good of the King
"and Kingdom. But his good Subjects would easily
"put the case to themselves. whether if the Papists
"in *Ireland* in truth were, or, by Art or Accident,
"had made themselves the Major part of both Hou-
"ses of Parliament there; and had pretended the
"Trust in that Declaration from the Kingdom of
"*Ireland*; thereupon, had Voted their Religion and

"Liberty to be in danger of extirpation from a Malignant Party of Protestants, and Puritans; and therefore, that they would put themselves into a posture of Defence; that the Forts, and the Militia of that Kingdom were to be put into the hands of such Persons, as they could Confide in; that his Majesty was indeed trusted with the Towns, Forts, Magazines, Treasures, Offices and People of the Kingdom, for the good, safety, and best advantage thereof; but as his Trust is for the use of the Kingdom, so it ought to be managed by the Advice of both Houses of Parliament; whom the Kingdom had trusted for that purpose, it being their duty to see it discharged according to the condition, and true intent thereof, and by all possible means to prevent the contrary: His Majesty said, let all his good Subjects consider, if that Rebellion had been plotted with all that formality, and those circumstances declared to be legal, at least according to the Equitable sense of the Law, and to be for the public good, and justifiable by necessity, of which They were the only Judges, whether, though they might have thought their design to be more Cunning, they would believe it the more Justifiable.

"Nay let the Framers of that Declaration ask themselves if the evil Counsellors, the Malignant Party, the Persons ill affected, the Popish Lords and their Adherents, should prove now, or hereafter, to be a Major part of both Houses (for it had been declared that a great part of both Houses had been such, and so might have been the Greater; Nay, the greater part of the House of Peers was still declared to be such, and his Majesty had not heard

OF THE REBELLION.

" of any of their conversion; and thereupon it had
" been earnestly pressed, that the Major part of the
" Lords might joyn with the Major part of the House
" of Commons) would his Majesty be bound to con-
" sent to all such alterations, as those Men should
" propose to him, and Resolve to be for the public
" Good: And should the Liberty, Property, and Se-
" curity of all his Subjects, depend on what such
" Votes should declare to be Law? Was the Order
" of the Militia unfit and unlawful, whilst the
" Major part of the Lords refused to join in it (as
" they had done two or three several times, and it
" was never heard, before this Parliament, that they
" should be so, and so often press'd after a Dissent de-
" clared) and did it grow immediately necessary for
" the public safety, and lawful by the Law of the
" Land, as soon as so many of the dissenting Peers
" were driven away (after their Names had been re-
" quired at the Bar, contrary to the freedom, and
" foundation of Parliament) that the other Opinion
" Prevailed? Did the Life, and Liberty of the Sub-
" ject depend upon such Accidents of days, and
" hours, that it was impossible for him to know his
" Right in either? God forbid.

" But now, to justify their Invasion of his Ma-
" jesty's ancient, unquestioned, undoubted Right,
" settled and established on his Majesty and his Pos-
" terity by God himself; confirmed, and streng-
" thened by all possible Titles of Compact, Laws,
" Oaths, perpetual and uncontradicted Custom, by
" his People; What had they alledged to declare to
" the Kingdom, as they say, the obligation that lieth

G 4

" upon the Kings of this Realm to pass all such Bills,
" as are offered unto them by both Houses of Parlia-
" ment? A thing never heard of till that day: An
" Oath (Authority enough for them to break all
" theirs) that is, or ought to be, taken by the Kings
" of this Realm, which is as well to remedy by Law
" such Inconveniences the King may suffer, as to
" keep, and protect the Laws already in being: And
" the Form of this Oath, they said, did appear upon
" a Record there cited; and by a Clause in the Pream-
" ble of a Statute, made in the 25th year or *Edw.* III.

" His Majesty said, he was not enough acquainted
" with Records to know whether that were fully,
" and ingenuously cited; and when, and how, and
" why, the several Clauses had been inserted, or
" taken out of the Oaths formerly administered to
" the Kings of this Realm: Yet he could not possibly
" imagine the assertion that Declaration made, could
" be deduced from the words, or the matter of that
" Oath: for unless they had a power of declaring
" Latin, as well as Law, sure, *elegeris*, signified *hath*
" chosen, as well as *will* chuse; and that it signified
" so there (besides the Authority of the perpetual
" Practice of all succeeding times: a better Inter-
" preter than their Votes) it was evident, by the
" reference it had to customs, *consuetudines quas vul-*
" *gus elegerit*: And could that be a Custom, which
" the People should chuse after this Oath taken?
" And should a King be sworn to defend such Cus-
" toms? Besides could it be imagined, that he should
" be bound by Oath to pass such Laws (and such a
" Law was the Bill they brought to him of the Mili-
" tia) as should put the power, wherewith he was

"trusted, out of Himself into the hands of other Men; and divert and disable himself of all possible power to perform the great business of the Oath; which was to protect them? If his Majesty gave away all his power, or if it were taken from him, he could not protect any Man: And what discharge would it be for his Majesty, either before God or Man, when his Good Subjects, whom God and the Law had committed to his charge, should be worried and spoiled, to say that he trusted others to protect them? That is, to do that Duty for him, which was essentially, and inseparably his own. But that all his good Subjects might see how faithfully these Men, who assumed this Trust from them, desired to discharge their Trust; he would be contented to publish for their satisfaction (a matter notorious enough, but what he himself never thought to have been put to publish, and of which the Framers of that Declaration might as well have made use, as of a Latin Record they knew many of his good Subjects could not, and many of themselves did not understand) the Oath itself he took at his Coronation, warranted and injoined to it by the Customs, and directions of his Predecessors; and the Ceremony of theirs, and his taking it; they might find it in the Records of the Exchequer; This it is:"

The Sermon being done, the Arch-Bishop goeth to the King, and asks his willingness to take the Oath usually taken by his Predecessors:

The King showeth himself willing, and goeth to the Altar; the Arch-Bishop administers these Questions, and the King Answereth them severally:

Episcopus. Sir, will you grant and keep, and by your Oath confirm to the People of *England*, the Laws and Customs to them granted by the Kings of *England*, your Lawful and Religious Predecessors: And namely the Laws, Customs, and Franchises granted to the Clergy, by the Glorious King Saint *Edward*, your Predecessor, according to the Laws of God, the true profession of the Gospel established in this Kingdom, and agreeable to the Prerogative of the Kings thereof, and the Ancient Customs of this Realm?

Rex. I grant, and promise to keep them.

Episc. Sir, will you keep Peace, and godly agreement entirely, according to your power, both to God, the Holy Church, the Clergy, and the People.

Rex. I will keep it.

Episc. Sir, will you to your Power, cause Law, Justice, and Discretion, in Mercy and Truth, to be executed in all your Judgments?

Rex. I will.

Episc. Sir, will you grant to hold, and keep the Laws, and rightful Customs, which the Commonalty of this your Kingdom have; and will you defend, and uphold them to the Honor of God, so much as in you lieth?

Rex. I grant, and promise so to do.

Then one of the Bishops reads this Admonition to the King, before the People, with a loud Voice.

OF THE REBELLION.

Our Lord and King, we beseech you, to pardon, and to grant, and to preserve unto us, and to the Churches committed, to our Charge, all Canonical Privileges, and due Law, and Justice; and that you would protect, and defend us, as every good King in his Kingdom ought to be Protector, and Defender of the Bishops, and Churches under their Government.

The King Answereth;

With a willing and devout Heart I promise, and grant my Pardon; and that I will preserve and maintain to you, and the Churches committed to your Charge, all Canonical Privileges, and due Law, and Justice, and that I will be your Protector and Defender, to my Power, by the assistance of God, as every good King in this Kingdom in right ought to protect, and defend the Bishops, and the Churches under their Government.

Then the King ariseth, and is led to the Communion-Table: where He makes a solemn Oath in sight of all the People, to observe the Premises; and, laying his Hand upon the Book, sayeth:

The OATH,

The things which I before promised, I shall perform, and keep: So help me God, and the Contents of this Book.

His Majesty said, "all the World might judge, "whether such Doctrine, or such Conclusions, as "those Men brought, could follow, or have the least "pretence, from that Oath; For the Preamble of

"the Statute they cited, that told his Majesty, that
"the King was bound to remedy, by Law, the
"mischiefs and damages which happen to his People:
"his Majesty said, he was so; but asked whether the
"King were bound, by the Preamble of that Statute,
"to renounce his own judgment, his own under-
"standing in those mischiefs, and of these remedies?
"How far forth he was obliged to follow the judge-
"ment of his Parliament, that Declaration still con-
"fessed to be a question. Without question, he
"said, none could take upon them to remedy even
"mischiefs, but by Law, for fear of greater mischiefs
"than those they go about to remedy.

"But his Majesty was bound in justice to consent
"to their Proposals, because there was a Trust repo-
"sed in his Majesty to preserve the Kingdom, by
"making new Laws: He said, he was glad there was
"so; then he was sure no new Law could be made
"without His Consent; and that the gentleness of
"his Answer, *le Roy S'avisera*, if it be no Denial, it
"is no Consent; and then the matter was not great.
"They would yet allow his Majesty a greater lati-
"tude of granting, or denying, as he should think
"fit, in public Acts of Grace, as Pardons, or the
"like Grants of Favor: Why did they so? If those
"Pardons, and public Acts of Grace were for the
"public Good (which they might Vote them to be)
"they would then be absolutely in their own dif-
"posal: But had they left that power to his Majesty?
"They had sure, at least, shared it with him; How
"else had they got the power to pardon Serjeant-
"Major-General *Skippon* (a new Officer of State,

"and a Subject his Majesty had no Authority to send
"to speak with) and all other Persons employed by
"them, and such as had employed themselves for
"them, not only for what they had done, but for
"what they should do? If they had power to declare
"such Actions to be no Treason, which his Majesty
"would not pardon; such Actions to be Treason,
"which need no pardon; the Latitude they allowed
"his Majesty of granting, or denying of Pardons,
"was a Jewel they might still be content to suffer his
"Majesty to wear in his Crown, and never think
"themselves the more in danger.

"All this considered, the Contriver of that Mes-
"sage (since they would afford his Majesty no better
"Title) whom they were angry with, did not con-
"ceive, the People of this Land to be so void of
"Common Sense, as to believe his Majesty, who had
"denied no one thing for the ease, and benefit of
"them, which in Justice or Prudence could be asked,
"or in Honor and Conscience could be granted, to
"have cast off all care of the Subject's Good; and
"the Framers, and Devisers of that Declaration
"(who had endeavoured to render his Majesty
"odious to his Subjects, and them disloyal to him,
"by pretending such a Trust in Them) to have only
"taken it up: Neither, he was confident, would
"they be satisfied, when they felt the misery and
"the burdens, which the fury and the malice of
"those People would bring upon them, with being
"told that calamity proceeded from evil Counsel-
"lors, whom no body could name; from Plots and
"Conspiracies, which no Man could discover; and

"from Fears and Jealousies, which no Man under-
"stood: And therefore, that the consideration of
"it should be left to the Conscience, Reason, Affec-
"tion, and Loyalty of his good Subjects, who do
"understand the Government of this Kingdom, his
"Majesty said, he was well content.

"His Majesty asked, where the folly and madness
"of those people would end, who would have his
"People believe, that his absenting himself from
"*London*, where, with his safety, he could not stay,
"and the continuing his Magazine at *Hull*, pro-
"ceeded from the secret Plots of the Papists here,
"and to advance the design of the Papists in *Ireland*?
"But it was no wonder that they, who could
"believe Sir *John Hotham*'s shutting his Majesty
"out of *Hull*, to be an Act of Affection and Loyalty,
"would believe that the Papists, or the Turk per-
"suaded him to go thither.

"And could any sober Man think that Declara-
"tion to be the consent of either, or both Houses of
"Parliament, unawed either by fraud or force;
"which (after so many Thanks, and humble Ac-
"knowledgments of his gracious favor in his Mes-
"sage of the twentieth of *January*, so often, and so
"unanimously presented to his Majesty from both
"Houses of Parliament) now told him, that the Mes-
"sage at first was, and, as often as it had been since
"mentioned by him, had been a breach of Privilege
"(of which they had not used to have been so negli-
"gent, as in four Months not to have complained, if
"such a breach had been) and that their own Method
"of proceeding should not be proposed to them;

"as if his Majesty had only Authority to call them
"together, not to tell them what they were to do,
"not so much as with reference to his own Affairs.
"What their own Method had been, and whither it
"had led Them, and brought the Kingdom, all
"Men see; what His would have been, if seasonably
"and timely applied unto, all Men might judge;
"his Majesty would speak no more of it.

"But see now what excellent Instances, they had
"found out, to prove an inclination, if not in his
"Majesty, in some about him, to Civil War: Their
"going with his Majesty to the House of Commons
"(so often urged, and so fully Answered) their at-
"tending on him to *Hampton* Court, and appearing
"in a Warlike manner at *Kingston* upon *Thames*;
"His going to *Hull*; their drawing their Swords at
"*York*, demanding, who would be for the King? the
"declaring Sir *John Hotham* Traytor, before the
"Message sent to the Parliament; the Propositions
"to the Gentry in *York-shire*, to assist his Majesty
"against Sir *John Hotham*, before he had received an
"Answer from the Parliament: All desperate Instan-
"ces of an inclination to a Civil War. Examine them
"again: The Manner, and Intent of his going to the
"House of Commons, he had set forth at large, in his
"Answer to their Declaration of the nineteenth of
"*May*; all Men might judge of it. Next, did they
"themselves believe, to what purpose soever that
"Rumor had served their turn, that there was an
"appearance in Warlike manner at *Kingston* upon
"*Thames*? Did they not know, that whensoever his
"Majesty had been at *Hampton*-Court, since his first

"coming to the Crown, there was never a less appearance, or in a less Warlike manner, than at the time they meant? He said, he would say no more, but that His appearance in a Warlike manner at *Kingston* upon *Thames*, and Theirs at *Kingston* upon *Hull*, was very different? What was meant by the drawing of Swords at *York* and demanding, who would be for the King, must be inquired at *London*; for, his Majesty believed, very few in *York* understood the meaning of it. For his going to *Hull*, which they would by no means endure should be called a Visit, whether it were not the way to prevent, rather than to make a Civil War, was very obvious: And the declaring him a Traytor in the very Act of his Treason, would never be thought unreasonable, but by those who believed him to be a loving, and loyal Subject; no more than the endeavouring to make the Gentlemen of that County sensible of that Treason (which they were in an honorable, and dutiful degree) before he received the Answer from both Houses of Parliament: For, if they had been, as his Majesty expected they should have been, sensible of that intolerable injury offered to him, might he not have had occasion to have used the affection of these Gentlemen? Was he sure that Sir *John Hotham*, who had kept him out without their Order (he spake of a public Order) would have let him in, when they had forbidden him? And if they had not such a sense of him (as the case fal out to be) had he not more reason to make Propositions to those Gentlemen, whose readiness and affection he, or his Posterity, would never forget? That

"But this business of *Hull* sticks still with them; and finding his Questions hard, they are pleased to Answer his Majesty by asking other Questions of Him: No matter for the exceptions against the Earl of *New-Castle* (which have been so often urged, as one of the principal grounds of their Fears and Jealousies; and which drew that Question from him) They asked his Majesty, why, when he held it necessary, that a Governor should be placed in *Hull*, Sir *John Hotham* should be refused by him, and the Earl of *New-Castle* sent down? His Majesty Answered, because he had a better opinion of the Earl of *New-Castle* than of Sir *John Hotham*; and desired to have such a Governor over his Towns, if he must have any, as should keep them for, and not against him: And if his going down were in a more private way than Sir *John Hotham's*, it was because he had not that Authority to make a noise by levying and billeting of Soldiers, in a peaceable time, upon his good Subjects, as it seemed Sir *John Hotham* carried down with him. And the Imputation which is cast by the way upon that Earl, to make his reputation not so unblemished, as he conceived, and the World believes it to be, and which, though it was not ground enough for Judicial Proceeding (it is wonder it was not) was yet ground enough for suspicion, must be the case of every Subject in *England* (and he wished it went no higher) if every vile Aspersion, contrived by unknown hands, upon unknown or unimaginable grounds, which is the way practised to bring any Virtuous and deserving Men into obloquy, "should receive the least credit, or countenance in the world.

"They tell him, their Exception to those Gentlemen, who delivered their Petition to him at *York*, was that they presumed to take the Style upon them of all the Gentry, and Inhabitants of that County; whereas, they say, so many more of as good Quality as themselves, of that County, were of another opinion; and have since, by their Petition to his Majesty, disavowed that Act. Their Information in that point, his Majesty said, was no better than it useth to be; and they would find, that neither the Number, or the Quality of those who have, or will disavow that Petition, was as they imagine; though too many weak Persons were misled (which they did, and would every day more and more understand) by the Faction, Skill, and Industry of that True Malignant Party, of which he did, and had reason to complain. They said, they had received no Petition of so strange a nature: What nature? Contrary to the Votes of both Houses: that is, they had received no Petition they had no mind to receive. But his Majesty had told them again, and all his good Subjects would tell them, that they had received Petitions, with joy and approbation, against the Votes of both Houses of their Predecessors, confirmed and established into Laws by the consent of his Majesty, and his Ancestors; and allowed those Petitions to carry the Style, and to seem to carry the Desires of Cities, Towns, and Counties, when, of either City, Town, or County, very few known, or considerable Persons, had been privy to such Petitions: whereas, in

" truth, the Petitions delivered to his Majesty, against
" which they except, carried not the Style of all,
" but some of the Gentry and Inhabitants; and im-
" plied no other consent, than such as went visibly
" along with it.

" But his Majesty was all this while in a mistake;
" the Magazine at *Hull* was not taken from him.
" Who told them so? They who assure them (and
" whom without breaking their Privileges they must
" believe) that Sir *John Hotham*'s shutting the Gates
" against his Majesty, and resisting his entrance with
" armed Men (though he thought it in defiance of
" him) was indeed in obedience to him, and his Au-
" thority; and for His Service, and the Service of
" the Kingdom. He was to let none in, but such as
" came with his Majesty's Authority, signified by
" both Houses of Parliament: himself and they had
" ordered it so. And therefore he kept his Majesty
" out, only till his Majesty or he himself might send
" for their Directions. His Majesty said, he knew
" not whether the Contrivers of that Declaration
" meant, that his good Subjects should so soon under-
" stand, though it was plain enough to be under-
" stood, the meaning of the King's Authority signified
" by both Houses of Parliament: But sure the world
" would now easily discern in what miserable case he
" had, by this time, been (it is bad enough as it is) if
" he had consented to their Bill, or to their Ordin-
" ance of the Militia, and given those Men power to
" have raised all the Arms of the Kingdom against
" him, for the Common Good, by his own Autho-
" rity: Would they not, as they had kept him from

"Hull, by this time have beaten him from *York*, and pursued him out of the Kingdom, in his own behalf? Nay might not this Munition, which is not taken from him, be employed against him; not against his Authority signified by both Houses of Parliament, but only to kill those ill Counsellors, the Malignant Party which is about him, and yet for His Good, for the Public Good (they would declare it so) and so no Treason within the Statute of 25. *E.* III? which, by their Interpretation, had left his Majesty, the King of *England*, absolutely less provided for, in point of safety, than the meanest Subject of the Kingdom: And every Subject of this Land (for whose security that Law was made, that they may know their duty, and their danger in breaking of it) may be made a Traytor when these Men please to say, he is so. But did they think That, upon such an Interpretation (upon pretence of Authority of Book-Cases and Precedents, which, without doubt, they would have cited, if they had been to their purpose) out of which nothing can result, but confusion to King and People, would find any credit with his good Subjects? And that so excellent a Law, made both for security of King and People, shall be so eluded, by an interpretation no Learned Lawyer in *England* would at this hour, he believed, set under his hand, notwithstanding the Authority of that Declaration; which, he hoped, shall bring nothing but Infamy upon the Contrivers of it?

"Now to their Privileges: Though it be true, they say, that their Privileges do not extend to Treason, Felony, or breach of the Peace, so as to exempt the

" Members from all manner of Process, and Trial;
" yet it doth privilege them in the way, or method of
" their Trial: the Cause must be first brought before
" Them, and Their consent asked, before you can
" proceed. Why then their Privileges extend as far
" in these Cases, as in any that are most unquestioned;
" for no Privilege whatsoever, exempts them from
" all manner of Process and Trial, if you first acquaint
" the House with it, and they give you leave to pro-
" ceed by those Processes, or to that Trial: But, by
" this Rule, if a Member of either House commit a
" Murder, you must by no means meddle with him,
" till you have acquainted that House of which he is
" a Member, and received their direction for your
" Proceeding, assuring yourself, he will not stir from
" that place where you left him, till you return with
" their consent; should it be otherwise, it would be
" in the power of every Man, under the pretence of
" Murder, to take one after another, and as many as
" he pleaseth; and so, consequently, bring a Parlia-
" ment to what he pleaseth, when he pleaseth. If a
" Member of either House shall take a Purse at *York*
" (he may as probably take a Purse from a Subject,
" as Arms against the King) you must ride to *Lon-*
" *don*, to know what to do, and He may ride with
" you, and take a new purse every Stage, and must
" not be apprehended, or declared a Felon, till you
" have asked that House of which he is a Member;
" should it be otherwise, it might be in every Man's
" power to accuse as many Members as he would of
" taking Purses; and so bring a Parliament, and so all
" Parliaments, to nothing. Would these Men be

"believed? And yet they make no doubt but every one who hath taken the Protestation, would defend this Doctrine with his Life and Fortune. Would not his Subjects believe, that they had imposed a pretty Protestation upon them; and that they had a very good end in the doing of it, if it obligeth them to such hazards, to such undertakings? Must they forget or neglect his Majesty's Person, Honor, and Estate, which, by that Protestation, they are bound to defend; and in some degree, do understand? And must they only venture their Lives and Fortunes to justify Privileges they know not, or ever heard of before? Or are they bound by that Protestation to believe, that the Framers of that Declaration have power to extend their own Privileges, as far as they think fit; and to contract his Majesty's Rights, as much as they please; and that they are bound to believe them in either, and to venture their Lives and Fortunes in that Quarrel?

"From declaring how mean a Person his Majesty is, and how much the Kingdom hath been mistaken in the understanding of the Statute of the 25. *E.* III. concerning Treason, and that all Men need not fear levying War against him, so they have Their Order to Warrant them; They proceed, in the Spirit of Declaring, to certify his Subjects in the mistakings, which, near one hundred and fifty years, have been received concerning the Statute of the 11. *Hen.* VII. *ch.* 1. (a Statute all good Subjects will read with Comfort) and tell them, that the serving of the King for the time being, cannot be meant of *Perkin Warbeck*, or of any that should call

"himself King; but such a One as is allowed, and
"received by the Parliament in the behalf of the King-
"dom: And was not his Majesty so allowed; How-
"ever, through a dark Mist of Words, and urging
"their old Privileges (which, he hoped, he had
"sufficiently Answered, and will be every day more
"confuted by the Actions of his good Subjects) they
"conclude, that those that shall guide themselves by
"the judgment of Parliament, which they say is their
"own, ought, whatsoever happen, to be secure, and
"free from all Account and Penalties, upon the
"ground and Equity of that very Statute: How far
"their own Chancellors may help them in that
"Equity, his Majesty knew not; but by the help of
"God and that good Law, He would allow no such
"Equity: So then, there is the Doctrine of that
"Declaration; and these are the Propositions of the
"Contrivers of it."

1. That they have an absolute Power of declaring the Law; and that whatsoever they declare to be so, ought not to be questioned by his Majesty, or any Subject: So that all right and safety of Him and his People, must depend upon Their pleasure.

2. That no Precedents can be limits to bound their Proceedings: So they may do what they please.

3. That the Parliament may dispose of any thing, wherein the King or Subject hath a Right, for the Public Good; that they, without the King, are this Parliament, and judge of this Public Good; and that his Majesty's consent is not necessary: So the Life and Liberty of the Subject, and all the good Laws made for the security of them, may be disposed of

and repealed by the Major part of both Houses at any time present, and by any ways and means procured so to be; and his Majesty had no power to protect them.

4. That no Member of either House ought to be troubled or meddled with for Treason, Felony, or any other Crime, without the Cause first brought before Them, that they may judge of the Fact, and Their Leave obtained to proceed.

5. That the Sovereign Power resides in both Houses of Parliament; and that his Majesty had no Negative Voice: So then his Majesty Himself must be subject to their Commands.

6. That the levying of Forces against the Personal Commands of the King, though accompanied with his Presence, is not levying War against the King; but the levying War against his Laws and Authority (which They have power to declare, and signify) though not against his Person, is levying War against the King: And that Treason cannot be committed against his Person, otherwise than as he is intrusted with the Kingdom, and discharging that Trust; and that They have a power to judge, whether he discharges that Trust or no.

7. That if they should make the highest Precedents of other Parliaments their Patterns, there would be no cause to complain of want of Modesty or Duty in them; that is, they may Depose his Majesty when they will, and are not to be blamed for so doing.

" And now (as if the mere publishing of their reso-
" lutions, would not only prevail with the People,
" but, in the instant, destroy all Spirit, and Courage
" in his Majesty to preserve his own right, and honor)

"they had since taken the boldness to assault him
"with certain Propositions: which they call the most
"necessary effectual means for the removing those
"Jealousies, and Differences between his Majesty.
"and his People; that is, that he would be content
"to divest himself of all his Regal rights, and digni-
"ties; be content with the Title of a King, and suffer
"Them, according to their discretion to govern
"Him, and the Kingdom, and to dispose of his
"Children. How suitable and agreeable this Doctrine,
"and these Demands were to the affection of his
"loving Subjects, under whose Trust these Men
"pretend to Say, and Do these monstrous things;
"and to design not only the ruin of his Person, but of
"Monarchy itself (which, he might justly say, was
"more than ever was offered in any of his Prede-
"cessors times; for though the Person of the King
"hath been sometimes unjustly Deposed, yet the
"Regal Power was never, before this time, struck at)
"he believes his good Subjects would find some way
"to let Them, and the World know: And, from
"this time, such who had been misled, by Their ill
"Counsels, to have any hand in the execution of the
"Militia, would see to what Ends their service was
"designed; and therefore if they should presume
"hereafter to meddle in it, they must expect, that
"he would immediately proceed against them as
"actual raisers of Sedition, and as Enemies to his
"Sovereign Power.

"His Majesty said, he had done. And should now
"expect the worst Actions these Men had power to
"commit against him; worse Words they could not

"give him: And he doubted not, but the Major
"part of both Houses of Parliament, when they
"might come together with their honor and safety
"(as well those who were surprised at the passing of
"it, and understood not the malice in it, and the
"confusion that must grow by it, if believed; as those
"who were absent, or involved) would so far resent
"the indignity offered to his Majesty, the dishonor
"to Themselves, and the mischief to the whole
"Kingdom, by that Declaration; that they would
"speedily make the foul Contrivers of it Instances
"of their exemplary Justice; and brand Them, and
"their Doctrine, with the marks of their perpetual
"Scorn and Indignation."

Whilst this Answer, and Declaration of his Majesty's was preparing and publishing, which was done with all imaginable haste, and to which they made no Reply till many Months after the War was begun, they proceeded in all their Counsels towards the lessening his Majesty both in Reputation, and towards the improving their own Interests. For the first, upon the advantage of their former Vote, of the King's Intention to levy War against his Parliament, in the end of *May* they published Orders, "That the Sheriffs of
"the adjacent Counties should hinder, and make stay
"of all Arms and Ammunition carrying towards
"*York*, until they had given notice thereof unto the
"Lords and Commons; and should have received
"Their further Direction; and that they should
"prevent the coming together of any Soldiers, Horse
"or Foot, by any Warrant of his Majesty, without
"Their Advice or Consent: Which they did, not

upon any opinion that there would be any Arms or Ammunition carrying to his Majesty, they having entirely possessed themselves of all his Stores; or that they indeed believed, there was any Commission or Warrant to raise Soldiers, which they well knew there was not; but that, by this means, their Agents in the Country (which many Sheriffs and Justices of Peace were; and most Constables, and Inferior Officers) might, upon this Pretence, hinder the resorting to his Majesty, which they did with that Industry, that few Persons, who foreseeing the design, of those Orders, did not decline the great Roads, and made not pretences of travelling to some other place, and travelled in any Equipage towards his Majesty, escaped without being stayed by such watches: And most that were so stayed, finding it to no purpose to attend the Resotion, or Justice of the Houses, who always commended the vigilance of their Ministers, and did not expect, they should be bound up by the Letter of their Orders, made shift to escape with their own Persons, and were contented to leave their Horses behind them; They who attended to be repaired by the Justice of the Houses, finding so many delays, and those delays to be so chargeable, and themselves exposed to so many Questions, and such an Inquisition, that they thought their Liberty a great prize, whatever they left behind them.

For the improving their Interest, and Dependance, though they had as much of the Affection of the City as could reasonably be expected; and by their exercise of the Militia, had united them in a firm Bond, the communication of Guilt; yet they well understood

BOOK V.

their true strength consisted in the Rabble of the People, for the greatest part of the substantial, and wealthy Citizens, being not of their Party, and except some Expedient were found out, whereby they might be involved, and concerned in their Prosperity or Ruin, they thought themselves not so much in truth possessed of that City, as they seemed to be. They had heard it said, that *Edward* the fourth of *England* recovered the City of *London*, and by that the Kingdom, by the vast Debts that he owed there; Men looking upon the helping of Him to the Crown, as the helping Themselves to their Money, which was else desperate. Upon this ground, they had taken the first opportunity of Borrowing great Sums of them, in the beginning of this Parliament; when the richest and best affected Men, upon a presumption that hereby the Scots Army would suddenly March into their own Country, and the English as soon be Disbanded, cheerfully furnished that Money. Upon this ground, they still forbore to repay those Sums, disposing what was brought in upon the Bills of Subsidy, and other public Bills, to other purposes. And now, to make themselves more sure of them, they Borrowed another Sum of 100,000l. of them, upon pretence of the great Exigences of *Ireland*; which was their two-edged Sword, to lead them into the Liberty of laying what Imputations, they thought most convenient for their purposes, upon the King and Queen; and to draw what Money they thought fit from the City; and served them now to another important end, to raise Soldiers; but that Service itself, in order to suppressing the Rebellion there, was not, in any degree, advanced.

Having, by thefe means, thus provided for their main Ends, they made the People believe, they were preparing Propofitions to fend to the King; and the People were yet fo Innocent as to believe, that they would never fend Propofitions that were not reafonable: For though the unufual Acts which had been done by the King, as the going to the Houfe of Commons, and demanding the Members there, had put them into as unufual apprehenfions; and thofe, by the warmth and heat of Declarations and Anfwers, had drawn from them, by degrees, another kind of Language, than had before been ufed; yet moft Men believed, when thofe Paffions were digefted, and that any Propofitions fhould be made by them (which the King had long called for and invited) that they could not but be fuch, as would open a door for that Affection, Confidence, Duty, and Truft, upon which the Peace of the Kingdom might be reafonably founded. And Propofitions they did fend to the King, in the beginning of *June*; which were prefented to his Majefty, with great Solemnity, by their Committee refident there; which, in this place, are very neceffary to be inferted in the very terms in which they were prefented, as followeth:

> The humble Petition, and Advice of both Houfes of Parliament, with Nineteen Propofitions and the Conclufion, fent unto his Majefty the fecond of June 1642.

The Nineteen Propofitions fent to the King by both Houfes June 2, 1642.

" Your Majefty's moft humble and faithful Subjects,
" the Lords and Commons in Parliament, having
" nothing in their thoughts and defires, more

"precious and of higher esteem, next to the
"Honor and immediate Service of God, than the
"just and faithful performance of their Duty to
"your Majesty, and this Kingdom: And being
"very sensible of the great distractions and dis-
"tempers, and of the Imminent dangers and
"calamities, which those distractions and distem-
"pers are like to bring upon your Majesty, and
"your Subjects (all which have proceeded from
"the subtle Informations, mischievous Practices,
"and evil Counsels of Men disaffected to God's
"true Religion; your Majesty's Honor and
"Safety; and the public Peace, and Prosperity
"of your People) after a serious Observation of
"the Causes of those mischiefs, do, in all humi-
"lity and sincerity, present to your Majesty their
"most dutiful Petition and Advice: That, out of
"your Princely Wisdom for the establishing your
"own Honor and Safety, and gracious tenderness
"of the Welfare and Security of your Subjects
"and Dominions, you will be pleased to grant,
"and accept these their humble Desires and Pro-
"positions, as the most necessary and effectual
"means, through God's blessing, of removing
"those Jealousies and Differences, which have
"unhappily fallen out betwixt you and your
"People, and procuring both your Majesty and
"Them, a constant course of Honor, Peace, and
"Happiness."

The Propositions.

1. "That the Lords and others of your Majesty's
"Privy-Council, and such great Officers and

" Ministers of State, either at Home or beyond
" the Seas, may be put from your Privy-Council,
" and from those Offices and Employments, ex-
" cepting such as shall be approved by both Hou-
" ses of Parliament: And that the Persons, put
" into the Places and Employments of those that
" are removed, may be approved of by both
" Houses of Parliament: and that Privy-Counsel-
" lors shall take an Oath, for the due execution of
" their Places, in such Form as shall be agreed
" upon by both Houses of Parliament.

2. " That the great Affairs of the Kingdom may not
" be concluded, or transacted by the Advice of
" private Men, or by any unknown, or unsworn
" Counsellors; but that such matters as concern
" the Public, and are proper for the High Court
" of Parliament, which is your Majesty's great
" and supreme Council, may be debated, resolved,
" and transacted only in Parliament, and not else-
" where: And such as shall presume to do any
" thing to the contrary, shall be reserved to the
" Censure and Judgment of Parliament: And such
" other Matters of State, as are proper for your
" Majesty's Privy-Council, shall be debated and
" concluded by such of the Nobility, and Others,
" as shall, from time to time, be chosen for that
" Place, by approbation of both Houses of Par-
" liament: And that no public Act concerning the
" Affairs of the Kingdom, which are proper for
" your Privy-Council, may be esteemed of any
" Validity, as proceeding from the Royal Autho-
" rity, unless it be done by the Advice and Consent

"of the Major part of the Council, attested
"under their Hands: And that your Council may
"be limited to a certain Number, not exceeding
"twenty-five, nor under fifteen; and if any
"Counsellor's place happen to be Void in the
"interval of Parliament, it shall not be supplied
"without the Assent of the Major part of the
"Council; which choice shall be confirmed at
"the next Sitting of Parliament, or else to be void.

3. "That the Lord High Steward of *England*, Lord
"High Constable, Lord Chancellor, or Lord
"Keeper of the Great Seal, Lord Treasurer, Lord
"Privy Seal, Earl Marshal, Lord Admiral,
"Warden of the Cinque Ports, chief Governor
"of *Ireland*, Chancellor of the Exchequer, Mas-
"ter of the Wards, Secretaries of State, two
"Chief Justices, and Chief Baron, may always
"be chosen with the approbation of both Houses
"of Parliament; and in the intervals of Parlia-
"ment, by the Assent of the Major part of the
"Council, in such manner as is before expressed
"in the choice of Counsellors.

4. "That He, or They, unto whom the Govern-
"ment and Education of the King's Children
"shall be committed, shall be approved of by
"both Houses of Parliament; and, in the inter-
"vals of Parliament, by the Assent of the Major
"part of the Council, in such manner as is before
"expressed in the choice of Counsellors; And
"that all such Servants as are now about them,
"against whom both Houses shall have any just
"Exceptions, shall be removed.

5. That

5. "That no Marriage shall be concluded, or
"treated, for any of the King's Children, with
"any Foreign Prince, or other Person what-
"soever, Abroad or at Home, without the Con-
"sent of Parliament, under the Penalty of a Præ-
"munire, unto such as shall conclude, or treat
"of any Marriage as aforesaid: And that the said
"Penalty shall not be pardoned, or dispensed
"with, but by the Consent of both Houses of
"Parliament.

6. "That the Laws in force against Jesuits, Priests,
"and Popish Recusants, be strictly put in Execu-
"tion without any Toleration, or Dispensation
"to the contrary: And that some more effectual
"course may be enacted, by Authority of Par-
"liament, to disable them from making any dis-
"turbance in the State; or eluding the Laws by
"Trusts, or otherwise.

7. "That the Votes of Popish Lords in the House of
"Peers may be taken away, so long as they con-
"tinue Papists: And that your Majesty will
"consent to such a Bill, as shall be drawn, for
"the Education of the Children of Papists, by
"Protestants, in the Protestant Religion.

8. "That your Majesty will be pleased to consent,
"that such a Reformation be made of the Church-
"Government, and Liturgy, as both Houses
"of Parliament shall advise; wherein they intend
"to have consultations with Divines, as is ex-
"pressed in their Declaration to that purpose:
"And that your Majesty will contribute your
"best assistance to them, for the raising of a suffi-

BOOK V.

"sufficient maintenance for Preaching Ministers
" through the Kingdom: And that your Majesty
" will be pleased to give your consent to Laws
" for the taking away of Innovations, and
" Superstition, and of Pluralities, and against
" scandalous Ministers.

9. " That your Majesty will be pleased to rest satis-
" fied with that course, that the Lords and Com-
" mons have appointed, for ordering of the
" Militia, until the same shall be further settled
" by a Bill: And that your Majesty will recal
" your Declarations, and Proclamations against
" the Ordinance made by the Lords and Com-
" mons concerning it.

10. " That such Members of either House of Parlia-
" ment, as have, during this present Parliament,
" been put out of any Place and Office, may
" either be restored to that Place and Office, or
" otherwise have satisfaction for the same, upon
" the Petition of that House, whereof He, or
" They are Members.

11. " That all Privy-Counsellors and Judges may
" take an Oath, the Form whereof to be agreed
" on and settled by Act of Parliament, for the
" maintaining of the Petition of Right, and of
" certain Statutes made by this Parliament, which
" shall be mentioned by both Houses of Parlia-
" ment: and that an inquiry of all Breaches, and
" Violations of those Laws, may be given in
" charge by the Justices of the King's Bench
" every Term, and by the Judges of Assize in
" their Circuits, and Justices of the Peace at the

"Sessions, to be presented and punished according to Law.

12. "That all the Judges, and all the Officers, placed by approbation of both Houses of Parliament may hold their places *quamdiu bene se gesserint.*

13. "That the Justice of Parliament may pass upon all Delinquents, whether they be within the Kingdom, or fled out of it: And that all Persons cited by either House of Parliament, may appear; and abide the Censure of Parliament.

14. "That the General Pardon, offered by your Majesty, may be granted with such Exceptions, as shall be advised by both Houses of Parliament.

15. "That the Forts, and Castles of this Kingdom, may be put under the Command and Custody of such Persons, as your Majesty shall appoint with the approbation of your Parliament; and in the intervals of Parliament, with approbation of the Major part of the Council, in such manner as is before expressed in the choice of Counsellors.

16. "That the extraordinary Guards, and Military Forces now attending your Majesty, may be removed and discharged; and that, for the future, you will raise no such Guards or extraordinary Forces, but, according to the Law, in case of Actual Rebellion, or Invasion.

17. "That your Majesty will be pleased to enter into a more strict Alliance with the States of the *United Provinces*, and other neighbour Princes and States of the Protestant Religion, for the defence and maintenance thereof against all Designs and

"Attempts of the Pope, and his Adherents, to "subvert and suppress it; whereby your Majesty "will obtain great access of strength and reputa- "tion, and your Subjects be much encouraged "and enabled, in a Parliamentary way, for your "Aid, and Assistance, in restoring your Royal "Sister, and her Princely Issue to those Dignities "and Dominions, which belong unto them; and "relieving the other distressed Protestant Princes, "who have suffered in the same Cause.

18. "That your Majesty will be pleased by Act of "Parliament, to clear the Lord *Kimbolton*, and the "five Members of the House of Commons, in such "manner that future Parliaments may be secured "from the Consequence of that evil Precedent.

19. "That your Majesty will be graciously pleased "to pass a Bill for restraining Peers made hereafter, "from Sitting or Voting in Parliament, unless "they be admitted thereunto with the Consent "of both Houses of Parliament.

"And these our humble Desires being granted by "your Majesty, We shall forthwith apply our- "selves to regulate your present Revenue, in such "sort as may be for your best advantage; and "likewise to settle such an ordinary, and constant "increase of it, as shall be sufficient to support "your Royal Dignity in Honor, and Plenty, "beyond the proportion of any former Grants of "the Subjects of this Kingdom to your Majesty's "Royal Predecessors: We shall likewise put the "Town of *Hull* into such hands, as your Majesty "shall appoint with the consent and approbation

OF THE REBELLION.

"of Parliament; and deliver up a just Account "of all the Magazine; and chearfully employ the "uttermost of Our power and endeavours, in the "real expression, and performance of our most "Dutiful and Loyal Affections, to the preserving "and maintaining the Royal Honor, Greatness, "and Safety of your Majesty, and your Posterity."

The same day that these Articles of Deposition were passed the Houses, that his Majesty might see how unable he was like to be to contend with them, they declared by an Order, the same day printed and carefully dispersed, "that they had received Infor- "mation" (and indeed their Informations were wonderful particular, from all parts beyond Sea, of whatsoever was agitated on the King's behalf; as well as from his Court, of whatsoever was designed, or almost but thought of to himself: Besides they could pretend to receive Information of whatsoever would any way conduce to their purpose, true or false) "that the Jewels of the Crown (which, they "said, by the Law of the Land ought not to be "aliened) were either pawned or sold in *Amsterdam*, "or some other parts beyond Seas; and thereby "great Sums of Money provided to be returned to "*York*, or to some of his Majesty's Servants or "Agents, for his Majesty's use: And because, they "said, it was more than probable that great pro- "vision of Moneys, in such an extraordinary way, "was to maintain the intended War against the "Parliament; and thereby to bring the whole King- "dom into utter ruin, and combustion: It was "therefore declared, by the Lords and Commons in

BOOK V.

Order of the two Houses.

I 3

"Parliament, that whosoever had been, or should be, an Actor in the selling or pawning of any Jewels of the Crown; or had, or should pay, lend, send, or bring any Money in Specie into this Kingdom for, or upon, any of those Jewels; or whosoever had, or should accept of any Bill from beyond the Seas for the payment of any Sum of Money, for or upon any of those Jewels, and should pay any Sum according to such Bill, after notice of that Order, without acquainting that House with the Receipt of that Bill, before he accept the same; or if he had already accepted any such Bill, then with the Acceptance thereof, before the payment of the Money, every such Person should be held and accounted a Promoter of that intended War, an Enemy to the State, and ought to give satisfaction for the public damage out of his own Estate."

Upon this confident Assumption, "that it was not in the King's power to dispose the Jewels of the Crown; that whatsoever Jewels were offered to be pawned or sold, by any of the King's Ministers beyond the Seas, were the Jewels of the Crown, and no other; and that all Money, returned from thence for his Majesty's Service, was Money so raised and procured;" they so much terrified Men of all Conditions, that the Queen, having, by the Sale of some of her own Jewels, and by her other Dexterity, procured some Money for the King's supply, could not in a long time find any means to transmit it. However, this made no impression upon the King's Resolution; and though it

OF THE REBELLION.

might have some influence upon Merchantly Men, yet it stirred up most Generous minds to an Indignation to the King's behalf; and was new Evidence, if there had wanted any, what kind of Greatness he was to expect from complying with such immodest, and extravagant Proposers.

The King was once Resolved to have returned no Answer to them upon those Propositions; but to let the People alone to judge of the unreasonableness of them, and of the Indignity offered to him in the delivery of them; and that was the reason of the short mention he made of them, in the close of his Declaration to theirs of the 26th of *May:* But he was afterwards persuaded to vouchsafe a further notice of them, there being some particulars Popular enough, and others, that, at the first View, seemed not altogether so derogatory to him, and so inconvenient to the People, as in truth they were; and that therefore it was necessary to let the People know, that whatsoever was reasonable, and might be beneficial to the Kingdom, had been, for the most part, before offered by his Majesty; and should all be readily granted by him; and so to unfold the rest to them, that they might discern their own Welfare, and Security, to be as much endangered by those Demands, as the King's Rights, Honor, and Dignity: So that, in a short time after he received them, he sent to the two Houses, and published to the Kingdom, his Answer to those Nineteen Propositions, whereof it will be sufficient to repeat some few Particulars:

" In which he first remembered them of their

BOOK V.

Of his Majesty's Answer to the Nineteen Propositions.

"method, they had observed in their Proceedings
"towards him: That they had first totally sup-
"pressed the known Laws of the Land, and denied
"His power to be necessary to the making New,
"reducing the whole to their own Declarations,
"and single Votes: That they had possessed them-
"selves of his Magazines, Forts, and Militia: That
"they had so awed his Subjects with Pursuivants,
"long chargeable Attendance; heavy Censures;
"illegal Imprisonments; that few of them durst offer
"to present their tenderness of his Majesty's Suffer-
"ings, their own just Grievances, and their sense
"of those Violations of the Law (the Birth right of
"every Subject of the Kingdom) though in an
"humble Petition to both Houses; and if any did,
"it was stifled in the Birth; called Sedition; and
"burned by the Common Hangman: That they had
"restrained the attendance of his Ordinary, and
"Necessary Household-Servants: and seized upon
"those small Sums of Money, which his Credit had
"provided to buy him Bread; with Injunctions that
"no Money should be suffered to be conveyed, or
"returned to his Majesty to *York*, or to any of his
"Peers, or Servants with him; so that, in effect
"they had blocked him up in that County: That
"they had filled the Ears of his People with Fears
"and Jealousies (though taken up upon trust) Tales
"of Skippers, Salt-Fleets, and such like; by which
"Alarms they might prepare them to receive such
"Impressions, as might best advance their Design,
"when it should be ripe. And now, it seemed, they
"thought his Majesty sufficiently prepared for those

OF THE REBELLION.

"bitter Pills; that he was in a handsome posture to
"receive those humble Desires; which, probably,
"were intended to make way for a Superfœtation
"of a yet higher Nature; for they did not tell him:
"This was All. He said, he must observe, that
"those Contrivers (the better to advance their true
"ends) in those Propositions, disguised, as much
"as they could, their Intents with a mixture of some
"things really to be approved by every honest
"Man; others, Specious and Popular; and some
"which were already granted by his Majesty: All
"which were cunningly twisted, and mixed with
"those other things of their main Design, of Am-
"bition and private Interest, in hope that, at the
"first View, every Eye might not so clearly discern
"them in their proper Colors.

"His Majesty said, if the 1, 2, 3. 4, 5. 9. 10. 15,
"16 19, Demands had been Writ, and Printed,
"in a Tongue unknown to his Majesty and his
"People, it might have been possible, that He,
"and They might have charitably believed the Pro-
"positions to be such, as might have been in order
"to the Ends pretended in the Petition; to wit, the
"Establishment of his Honor and Safety; the Wel-
"fare and Security of his Subjects and Dominions,
"and the removing those Jealousies and Differences,
"which were said to have unhappily fallen betwixt
"his Majesty and his People; and procuring both
"his Majesty, and Them, a constant course of
"Honor, Peace, and Happiness; but being read
"and understood by all, he could not but assure
"Himself, that that Profession, joined to those

"Propositions, would rather appear a Mokery;
"and a Scorn; the Demands being such, that he
"were unworthy the Trust reposed in him by the
"Law, and of his Descent from so many Great and
"Famous Ancestors, if he could be brought to
"abandon that Power, which alone could enable
"him to perform what he was Sworn to, in protect-
"ing his People, and the Laws; and so assume
"others into it, as to divest Himself of it, although
"not only his present Condition were more Ne-
"cessitous than it was (which it could hardly be) and
"he were both Vanquished, and a Prisoner, and in
"a worse Condition than ever the most unfortunate
"of his Predecessors had been reduced to, by the
"most Criminal of their Subjects; and though the
"Bait laid to draw him to it, and to keep his Sub-
"jects from Indignation at the mention of it, the
"Promises of a plentiful and unparalleled Revenue,
"were reduced from Generals (which signify no-
"thing) to clear and certain Particulars; since such
"a bargain would have but too great a resemblance
"of that of *Esau*'s, if he would part with such flow-
"ers of his Crown, as were worth all the rest of
"the Garland, and had been transmitted to him
"from so many Ancestors, and had been found so
"useful and necessary for the Welfare and Security
"of his Subjects, for any present Necessity, or for
"any low and sordid Considerations of Wealth and
"Gain. And therefore, all Men knowing that
"those Accommodations are most easily made, and
"most exactly observed, that are grounded upon
"reasonable and equal conditions, his Majesty had

"great cause to believe that the Contrivers of those
"Propositions, had no Intention of settling any
"firm Accommodation, but to increase those Jea-
"lousies, and widen that Division, which, not by
"his Majesty's fault, was now unhappily fallen be-
"tween Him and both Houses.

"It was asked, that all the Lords and others of
"his Privy-Council, and such great Officers and
"Ministers of State, either at home or beyond the
"Seas (for, he said, care was taken to leave out
"no Person, or Place, that his dishonor might
"be sure not to be bounded within this Kingdom)
"should be put from his Privy-Council, and from
"those Offices and Employments, unless they should
"be approved by both Houses of Parliament, how
"faithful soever his Majesty had found them to
"Him, and to the Public; and how far soever
"they had been from offending against any Law,
"the only Rule they had, or any Others ought to
"have, to walk by. His Majesty therefore to that
"part of that Demand returned this Answer, That
"he was willing to grant, that they should take a
"larger Oath, than they Themselves desired in
"their eleventh Demand, for maintaining not of
"any Part, but the Whole Law. And, he said,
"he had, and did assure them, that he would be
"careful to make Election of such Persons in those
"Places of Trust, as had given good Testimonies
"of their Abilities and Integrities, and against whom
"there could be no just cause of Exception, where-
"on reasonably to ground a Diffidence: That if he
"had, or should be mistaken in his Election, he

BOOK V.

"had, and did assure them, that there was no Man
"so near to him, in Place or Affection, whom he
"would not leave to the Justice of the Law, if
"they should bring a particular Charge, and suffi-
"cient Proof against him: That he had given them
"a Triennial Parliament (the best pledge of the
"Effects of such a Promise on His part, and the best
"Security for the performance of their Duty on
"Theirs) the apprehension of whose Justice, would
"in all probability, make Them wary how they
"provoked it; and his Majesty wary, how he chose
"such as, by the discovery of their faults, might
"in any degree seem to discredit his Election; but
"that without any shadow of a fault objected, only
"perhaps because they follow their Consciences,
"and preserve the established Laws, and agree not
"in such Votes, or assent not to such Bills, as some
"Persons, who had then too great an influence
"even upon both Houses, judged, or seemed to
"judge, to be for the public good, and as were
"agreeable to that new Utopia of Religion and
"Government, into which they endeavoured to
"transform this Kingdom (for, he said, he remem-
"bered what Names, and for what Reasons, they
"left out in the Bill offered him concerning the
"Militia, which they had themselves recommended
"in the Ordinance) he would never consent to the
"displacing of any, whom for their former Merits
"from, and Affection to his Majesty and the
"Public, he had intrusted; since, he conceived,
"that to do so, would take away both from the
"Affection of his Servants, and care of his Service,

"and the Honor of his Justice: And, he said, he
" the more wondered, that it should be asked by
" them, since it appears by the twelfth Demand,
" that Themselves counted it reasonable, after the
" present Turn was served, that the Judges and
" Officers, who were then placed, might hold
" their Places, *quamdiu se bene gesserint*: And he
" was Resolved to be as careful of those whom He
" had chosen; as they were of those They would
" chuse; and to remove none, till they appeared
" to him to have otherwise behaved themselves,
" or should be evicted, by Legal Proceedings, to
" have done so.

" But, his Majesty said, that Demand, as un-
" reasonable as it was, was but one Link of a great
" Chain, and but the first Round of that Ladder, by
" which his Majesty's Just, Ancient, Regal Power,
" was endeavoured to be fetched down to the
" ground; for it appeared plainly that it was not
" with the Persons now chosen, but with his Ma-
" jesty's Chusing, that they were displeased: For
" they demanded, that the Persons put into the
" Places and Employments of those, who should
" be removed, might be approved by both Houses;
" which was so far from being less than the power
" so Nomination, that of two things, of which he
" would never grant either, he would sooner be
" content, that They should Nominate, and He
" Approve; than They Approve and his Majesty
" Nominate; the mere Nomination being so far
" from being any thing, that if he could do no More,
" he would never take the pains to do That; when

"he should only hazard whom he esteemed to the "Scorn of a Refusal, if they happened not to be "agreeable not only to the Judgment, but to the "Passion, Interest, or Humor of the present Major "part of either House: Not to speak of the great "Factions, Animosities, and Divisions, which "that Power would introduce in both Houses, and "in the several Counties for the choice of Persons "to be sent to that place, where that Power was; "and between the Persons that were so chosen. "Neither was that strange Potion prescribed to him "only for once, for the Cure of a present, pressing, "desperate Disease; but for a Diet to Him, and his "Posterity. It was demanded, that his Counsel- "lors, all Chief Officers both of Law and State, "Commanders of Forts and Castles, and all Peers "hereafter made, be Approved of, that is Chosen, "by Them from time to time: And rather than it "should ever be left to the Crown (to whom it "only did, and should belong) if any place fall void "in the intermission of Parliament, the Major part "of the approved Council was to approve them. "Neither was it only demanded that his Majesty "should quit the Power, and Right, his Predeces- "sors had had of appointing Persons in those Places; "but for Counsellors, he was to be restrained, as "well in the Number as in the Persons; and a "power must be annexed to those Places, which "their Predecessors had not. And indeed, if that "power were passed to them, he said, it would "not be fit He should be trusted to chuse those who "were to be trusted as much as Himself.

" He told them, to grant their Demands in the
" manner they proposed them, that all matters
" that concerned the Public, &c. should be resolved,
" and transacted only in Parliament, and such other
" matters of State, &c. by the Privy-Council so
" chosen, was in effect at once to depose Himself,
" and his Posterity. He said, many expressions in
" their Demands, had a greater Latitude of signifi-
" cation, than they seemed to have; and that it
" concerned his Majesty therefore the more, that
" they should speak out; that both He, and his
" People, might either know the bottom of their
" Demands, or know them to be bottomless. No-
" thing more concerned the Public, and was indeed
" more proper for the high Court of Parliament, than
" the making of Laws; which not only ought there to
" be transacted, but could be transacted no where else.
" But then they must admit his Majesty to be a part
" of the Parliament; they must not (as the sense was
" of that part of that Demand, if it had any) deny the
" freedom of his Answer, when He had as much
" right to reject what he thought unreasonable,
" as They had to propose what they thought con-
" venient, or necessary. Nor was it possible his
" Answers, either to Bills or any other Proposi-
" tions, should be wholly free, if he might not
" use the liberty, that every one of Them, and
" every Subject took, to receive Advice (without
" their danger who should give it) from any Person
" known or unknown, sworn or unsworn, in those
" matters in which the manage of his Vote is trusted,
" by the Law, to his own Judgment and Conscience;

BOOK V.

"which how best to inform was, and ever should be, left likewise to Him. He said, he would always, with due consideration, weigh the Advices both of his Great, and Privy-Council, yet he should likewise look on their Advices, as Advices, not as Commands, or Impositions, upon Them, as his Counsellors, not as his Tutors, or Guardians; and upon Himself, as their King, not as their Pupil, or Ward: For, he said, whatsoever of Regality was, by the modesty of Interpretation, left in his Majesty, in the first part of the second Demand, as to the Parliament, was taken from him, in the second part of the same, and placed in that new-fangled kind of Counsellors, whose power was such, and so expressed by it, that in all Public Acts concerning the Affairs of the Kingdom, which are proper for the Privy-Council (for whose Advice all Public Acts are sometimes proper, though never necessary) they were desired to be admitted joint Patentees with his Majesty in the Regality. And it was not plainly expressed, whether they meant his Majesty so much as a single Vote in those Affairs; but it was plain they meant him no more, at most, than a single Vote in them; and no more power, than every one of the rest of his fellow Counsellors."

And so after a sharp discourse, and explanation of the unreasonableness of the several Demands, or the greatest part of them, and the confusion that, by consenting thereunto, would redound to the Subject in general, as well as the dishonor to his

Majesty

Majesty (which may be read at large by itself) He told them, "to all those unreasonable Demands, "his Answer was, *nolumus Leges Angliæ mutari*: "But renewed his Promise to them, for a very "punctual and strict observation of the known Laws "established; to which purpose he was willing an "Oath should be framed by them, and taken by "all his Privy-Counsellors. And for any Alteration "in the Government of the Church, that a National "Synod should be called, to propose what should "be found necessary or convenient: And that for "the advancement of the Protestant Religion against "the Papists, they had not proposed so much to "his Majesty, as he was willing to grant, or as he "had himself offered before. He concluded with "conjuring Them, and all Men, to rest satisfied "with the truth of his Majesty's Professions, and "the reality of his Intentions; and not to ask such "things as denied themselves: That they would "declare against Tumults, and punish the Authors: "That they would allow his Majesty his Property "in his Towns, Arms, and Goods; and his share "in the Legislative Power; which would be counted "in Him not only breach of Privilege, but Tyranny, "and Subversion of Parliaments, to deny to them: "And, when they should have given him satisfaction "upon those Persons, who had taken away the "One, and recalled those Declarations (particularly "that of the 26ʰ of *May*; and those in the point of "the Militia, his just rights wherein he would no "more part with, than with his Crown, lest he "enabled others by them to take that from him) "which would take away the Other; and declined "the beginnings of a War against his Majesty, un- "der pretence of His intention of making one against "Them; as he had never opposed the First part of "the thirteenth Demand, so he would be ready to "concur with them in the Latter; and being then "confident that the credit of those Men, who desire "a general combustion, would be so weakened "with them, that they would not be able to do this "Kingdom any more hurt, he would be willing to "grant his General Pardon, with such Exceptions "as should be thought fit; and should receive much "more joy in the hope of a full, and constant hap- "piness of his People in the true Religion, and "under the protection of the Law, by a blessed "union between his Majesty and his Parliament, "than in any such increase of his own Revenue, "how much soever beyond former Grants, as (when "his Subjects were wealthiest) his Parliament could "have settled upon his Majesty."

Though the King now lived at *York* in a much more Princely condition, than he could have hoped to have done near *London*; and had so great a train and resort of the Nobility and Gentry, that there was not left a fifth part of the House of Peers at *Westminster*; and truly I do not believe, that there was near a Moiety of the House of Commons who continued there; yet his Majesty made no other use, for the present, of their presence with Him, and of their absence from the two Houses, than to have so many the more, and the more credible Witnesses of his Counsels and Carriage; and to undeceive the

People by his clear Anfwers to all the Scandals and Reproaches which were laid on him, and by his ample profeffions and proteftations of his fincere Zeal to Religion, and Juftice; and to make it appear to them, how far the Quality and the Number of thofe who thought, or feemed to think otherwife, was, from what they might imagine it to be. And it cannot be denied, but the People were every day vifibly reformed in their underftandings, from the fuperftitious reverence they had paid the two Houfes; and grew fenfible of their duty to the King, and of thofe Invafions which were offered to his Regal dignity.

On the other fide, the two Houfes flackened not their pace a jot, proceeded with great and unufual fharpnefs againft thofe Members who were gone to the King; Proclaiming fome of them by Name "to be Enemies to the Kingdom," and, by a Formal Judgment, fentencing Nine Peers together, "to be incapable of fitting again in Parliament, whilft This fhould continue:" The Houfe of Commons having carried up an Impeachment of Mifdemeanours againft them (which was as illegal in point of Juftice, and as extravagant in point of Privilege, as any thing they could do) "for being abfent, and refufing to attend, upon a Summons from the Houfe of Peers:" And upon their own Members they impofed a fine of 100l a piece, on every one who was gone to the King, and upon thofe, who being in other places, they thought were well affected to his Service: Yet, left they fhould upon this proceeding return again, to difturb, and crofs their

BOOK V.

Counsels, they provided, "that no Man upon whom "that Sentence fell, should sit again in the House "(though he paid his fine) till he had been examined "by a Committee, and so given the House satisfac- "tion in the cause of his absence." And, by those means, they thought both to remove the Scandal, that so many Members were absent, and to prevent any inconvenience too, that might befal them by their return. For they well knew, if the Members of both Houses were obliged to a constant and strict Attendance, it would not be possible that they could compass their mischievous Designs.

Propositions, and Orders of both Houses for bringing in Money and Plate for maintaining Horse, &c. June 10. 1642.

Then they prosecuted their great Business of the Militia, not only near *London*, where they were in no danger of opposition, but in those Northern Counties near his Majesty, as *Leicestershire, Cheshire, Lincolnshire*, where whosoever refused to give obedience to them, or published the King's Proclamation against their proceedings (for the King had yet practised no Expedient to prevent the growth of that mischief, but the publishing his Proclamation against it) were sent for as Delinquents; and not satisfied herewith, that they might be as well able to Pay an Army, as they found they should be to Raise one, on the tenth of *June* (for the time will be very necessary to be remembered, that it may be the better stated, Who took up the Defensive Arms) they published Propositions, "for the bring-
"ing in of Money or Plate to maintain Horse,
"Horsemen, and Arms, for the preservation of
"the Public Peace, and for the defence of the King
"and both Houses of Parliament; the Reasons and

"Grounds whereof they declared to be the King's
"Intention to make War against his Parliament,
"That, under pretence of a Guard for his Person,
"he had actually begun to levy Forces, both of
"Horse and Foot; and sent out Summons through-
"out the County of *York*, for the calling together
"of greater Numbers; and some ill affected Persons,
"in other parts, had been employed to raise Troops,
"under the color of his Majesty's Service; making
"large offers of reward and preferment to such as
"would come in: That his Majesty did, with a
"high and forcible hand, protect, and keep away
"Delinquents, not permitting them to make their
"appearance to Answer such Affronts and Injuries,
"as had been by them offered to the Parliament;
"and those Messengers, which had been sent from
"the Houses for them, had been abused, beaten,
"and imprisoned, so as the Orders of Parliament,
"the highest Court of Justice in the Realm, were
"not obeyed; and the Authority of it was altogether
"scorned, and vilified; and such Persons as stood
"well affected to it, and declared themselves sensible
"of those public Calamities, and of the violations
"of the Privileges of Parliament, and Common-
"Liberty of the Subject, were baffled, and injured
"by several sorts of Malignant Men, who were
"about the King; some whereof, under the name
"of Cavaliers, without having respect to the Laws
"of the Land, or any fear either of God or Man,
"were ready to commit all manner of Outrage and
"Violence; which must needs tend to the dissolu-
"tion of the Government; the destruction of their

"Religion, Laws, Liberties, Properties; all which would be exposed to the Malice and Violence of such desperate Persons, as must be employed in so horrid and unnatural an Act, as the overthrowing a Parliament by Force; which was the support, and preservation of them. Those Particulars, they said, being duly considered by the Lords and Commons, and how great an obligation lay upon them, in Honor, Conscience, and Duty, according to the high Trust reposed in them to use all possible means, in such cases, to prevent so great and irrecoverable Evils, they had thought fit to publish their sense, and apprehension of that Imminent danger; thereby to excite all well affected Persons, to contribute their best assistance, according to their solemn Vow and Protestation, to the Preparations necessary for the opposing, and suppressing of the Trayterous Attempts of those wicked, and malignant Counsellors, who sought to engage the King in so dangerous and destructive an enterprise, and the whole Kingdom in a Civil War; and destroy the Privileges and Being of Parliaments.

"This recourse to the good affections of those, that tender their Religion and just Liberties, and the enjoyment of the blessed fruits of this present Parliament, which were almost ready to be reaped, and were now as ready to be ruined by those wicked hands, being, they said, the only remedy left them under God; and without which they were no longer able to preserve Themselves, or Those by whom they were intrusted: Therefore, they declared that whosoever would bring in any

" proportion of ready Money or Plate, or would
" underwrite to furnish and maintain any number of
" Horse, Horsemen, and Arms, for the preserva-
" tion of the Public Peace, and for the defence of
" the King, and both Houses of Parliament, from
" Force and Violence, and to uphold the Power
" and Privileges of Parliament according to his Pro-
" testation; it should be held a good and acceptable
" Service to the Common-wealth, and a Testimony
" of his good affection to the Protestant Religion,
" the Laws, Liberties, and Peace of the Kingdom;
" and to the Parliament, and Privileges thereof.
" And they further declared, that whosoever brought
" in Money or Plate, or furnished and maintained
" Horse, Horsemen, and Arms, upon these Pro-
" positions, and to those Purposes, should be repaid
" their Money with interest of eight *per Cent*; for
" which they did engage the public Faith, and they
" appointed the Guild-Hall in *London* for the place
" whither this Money, or Plate, should be brought;
" and four Aldermen of *London* to be their Treasu-
" rers for the receiving the same; and likewise other
" Confiding Men to receive, and prize such Horses
" and Arms, as should be brought in for their
" Service. And lastly, for their better encourage-
" ment, the Members of both Houses appointed a
" solemn day to set down their own Subscriptions;
" which they performed liberally."

Most of those who abhorred their impious Designs, not thinking it lawful for them to be present at such Consultations, withdrew before the day came, or absented themselves Then. But many had the courage to be present, and stoutly to refuse what they thought they could not honestly consent to. Sir *Henry Killigrew*, who was a remarkable Enemy to all their devices, being called upon, told them, "if there were occasion, he would provide a good Horse, and a good Sword; and made no question but he should find a good Cause." But, within very few days both He, and all those who were taken notice of for refusing, found it safest for them to leave the Town; there being very visibly great animosity against them both within, and without the Walls. And a Gentleman of good Quality assured me afterwards, that, within few days after he had refused to Subscribe, he was privately advised by one of the other Faction, who yet retained some kindness to him, "to leave the Town, lest his Brains were beaten out by the Boys in the Streets." And many of those who too impotently desired not to be looked upon as Refractory Persons, and had pleased themselves with Subscribing more Articulately for the defence of the King's Person, found it afterwards necessary to supply whatsoever they had Subscribed, to be employed that way as was Declared to be for the defence of the King's Person, whatsoever their Intention was at first, or their Opinion after. And it is hardly credible, what a vast proportion of Plate was brought in to their Treasurers within ten days; there being hardly Men enough to receive it, or room to lay it in; and the Throng being so great of the Bringers, that, in two days attendance, many could not be discharged of their Seditious Offerings. And, the very next day after these

Propositions, they further ordered, "that there "should be a strict search and examination made, "by the Justices of Peace, Mayors, Bailiffs, and "Constables, near all the Northern Roads, for the "seizing all Horses for service in the Wars, or "great Saddles, that should be carried towards the "North parts of *England*, without the Privity or "Direction of one or both Houses of Parliament;" which was a great improvement of their former Order, which extended only to Arms and Ammunition; though, the truth is, the Dexterity and Spirit of their Ministers, who knew their Meaning, made the former almost as inconvenient and dangerous to Passengers, as the latter.

It was by many impatiently wondered at Then, and, no doubt, will be more censured Hereafter, that, notwithstanding all these invasions, and breaches upon the Regal Power, and all these vast Preparations to destroy him, the King, hitherto, put not himself into a posture of safety; or provided for the resistance of that Power, which threatened him; and which, he could not but know, Intended whatsoever it hath since Done; And though they had not yet formed an Army, and chosen a General, yet, he well knew, they had Materials abundantly ready for the first, and particular, digested resolutions, in the second; which they could reduce to public acts, whensoever they pleased. It is very true he did know all this, and the unspeakable hazards he run, in not preparing against it. But the hazards, which presented themselves unto him on the other side, were not less Prodigious: He had a very great appearance of the Nobility; and not only of those, who had from the beginning walked, and governed themselves by the Rules the Law prescribed, and, in that respect, were unblamable to King and People: But of Others who had passionately and peevishly (to say no worse) concurred in all the most violent Votes and Actions, which had been done from the beginning: For besides the Lord *Spencer* (who had been chosen their Lieutenant of *Northamtonshire*, but was recovered to a right understanding, of which he was very capable, by his Uncle the Earl of *Southampton*) the Lord *Paget* likewise, who had contributed all his Faculties to Their service, and to the prejudice of the King's, from before the beginning of the Parliament; had been one of their Teizers to broach those bold high Overtures soberer Men were not, at first, willing to be seen in; and had been, as a Man most worthy to be Confided in, chosen Lord Lieutenant of one of the most Confiding Counties, the County of *Buckingham* (where he had, with great Solemnity and Pomp, executed their Ordinance, in defiance of the King's Proclamation) and had Subscribed a greater number of Horses for their Service, upon their Propositions, than any other of the same Quality; convinced in his conscience, fled from them, and besought the King's Pardon: And, for the better manifesting the tenderness of his Compunction, and the horror he had of his former Guilt, he frankly discovered whatsoever he had known of their Counsels; and aggravated all the ill they had done, with declaring it to be done to worse and more horrid Ends, than many good Men believed to be possible for them to propose to themselves.

OF THE REBELLION.

Notwithstanding, this glorious Convention was rather an Ornament to his Court, than any great Advantage to his Counsels; and the use of them more to discredit the small remainder at *Westminster*, and that the People might see the number and quality of the Dissenters, than that they contrived any thing to the active improvement of his affairs; every Man thinking it high merit in him, that he absented himself from the Company and Place, where all the mischief was done: and that the keeping himself Negatively innocent, was as much as he owed his King and Country. I am willing to impute it to the drowsy and unactive Genius of the Kingdom (contracted by long ease, and quiet) which so much abhorred the thoughts of a Civil War, that it thought a lively and vigorous preparation against it, was to invite it; and there were very few of all the great Lords, who did attend upon the King, who did not declare, " that the Parliament durst not in truth " (whatever shows they made in hope to shake his " Majesty's constancy) make a War; and if they " should attempt it, the People would unanimously " rise for the King, who would be most safe by " not intending his own safety. Whereas, if he " raised Forces, the Parliament would procure them-" selves to be believed, that it was to overthrow " Religion, and suppress the Laws, and Liberties " of the People." They who were of another opinion, and could have spoken more reason, held it not safe to express themselves but in the King's own Ear; there being in the great Council of the Peers, who, for state, were frequently Assembled, and by

whom in truth the King then defired to have tranf-
acted all things of Moment, fome who were not
good Counfel-Keepers, and others who were looked
upon, and believed to be Spies upon the reft. But
that which made the thought of raifing Forces (whatever Arguments there were for it) abfolutely un-
reafonable, was, that the King had no poffibility to
procure either Arms, or Munition, but from *Holland*; from whence he daily expected fupply: And
till that arrived, let his Provocations and Sufferings
be what they could be, he was to fubmit and bear
it patiently.

In the mean time, for a ground of further proceeding upon occafion, the King defired the Peers in
Council, to fet down in writing the Affronts, and
Violence, which had been offered to them at *London*,
by which their Prefence in the great Council of the
Kingdom was rendered both unfafe, and difhonorable; the which they the more willingly conde-
fcended to, for that the *London* Pamphlets already
afperfed them, as Deferters of the Parliament, and
Betrayers of the Liberty of their Country: An In-
ftrument being drawn up and agreed upon between
them, in which they fet down " the Tumults, and
" the Violence offered to particular Perfons in thofe
" Tumults; the Threats and Menaces of the Rabble,
" at the doors of the Houfe, when they had a mind
" any Exorbitant thing fhould pafs; the Breach
" and Violation of the old Orders, and Rules of Par-
" liament, whilft Matters were in debate, and the
" refuming Matters again in a thin Houfe; and re-
" verfing, waving, or contradicting Refolutions

"made in a full House: And, lastly, Mr. *Hollis*'s
" coming to the Bar, and demanding the Names of
" those Lords who refused to consent to the Militia,
" when the multitude without menaced and threa-
" tened all those Dissenters:" after which, they said,
" they conceived, they could not be present there,
" with Honor, Freedom, or Safety; and therefore
" forbore to be any more present; and so all those
" Votes, Conclusions, and Declarations had passed,
" which had begot those Distractions throughout
" the Kingdom." And this they delivered to the
King, signed under their Hands. And yet (which
is a sufficient Instance how unendued Men were
with that Spirit and Courage, which was requisite)
the next day after the delivery, many Lords came to
his Majesty, and besought him " that he would by
" no means publish that Paper, but keep it in his
" own hands" some of them saying, " that, if it
" were published, they would disavow it:" so that
material and weighty Evidence, which Then might
have been of Sovereign use to the King, was rendered utterly ineffectual to his Service; his Majesty
finding it necessary to engage his Princely word to
them, " never to make it public without Their con-
" sent;" which he performed most punctually; and
so, to this day, it was never divulged.

To make some little amends for this want of mettle
(for it proceeded from nothing else, They being
most shy in subscribing, and most passionate against
publishing, who were of unquestionable Affection
to his Majesty, and integrity to his Cause) and that
the World might see, there was a Combination

BOOK V.

His Majesty's Declaration to the Lords attending him at York, June 13. 1642.

among good Men, to assist his Majesty in the defence of the Law, as well as there was against both by Others: Upon the King's declaring himself fully in Council, where all the Peers were present, "That, "as He would not require or exact any obedience "from them, but what should be warranted by the "known Law of the Land; so he did expect that "They would not yield to any Commands not legally grounded, or imposed by any other: That "he would defend every one of them, and all such "as should refuse any such Commands, whether "they proceeded from Votes, and Orders of both "Houses, or any other way, from all dangers and "hazards whatsoever. That his Majesty would defend the true Protestant Religion, established by "the Law of the Land; the Lawful Liberties of "the Subjects of *England*; and just Privileges of all "the Three Estates of Parliament; and would require no further Obedience from them, than as "accordingly he should perform the same: And his "Majesty did further declare, that he would not, "as was falsely pretended, engage them, or any of "them, in any War against the Parliament; except "it were for his necessary defence and safety, against "such as did insolently Invade or Attempt against "his Majesty, or such as should adhere to his Majesty:"

The promise of the Lords and others thereupon.

All the Peers engaged themselves, "not "to obey any Orders, or Commands whatsoever, "not warranted by the known Laws of the Land; "and to defend his Majesty's Person, Crown, and "Dignity, together with his Just and Legal Prerogative, against all Persons and Power whatsoever:

" That they would defend the true Proteſtant Reli-
" gion, eſtabliſhed by the Law of the Land; the
" Lawful Liberties of the Subject of *England*; and
" juſt Privileges of his Majeſty, and both his Houſes
" of Parliament: And laſtly, They engaged them-
" ſelves not to obey any Rule, Order, or Ordinance
" whatſoever, concerning any Militia, that had not
" the Royal Aſſent."

This being Subſcribed by their Lordſhips, was, with their conſent, immediately Printed, and carefully divulged over the Kingdom, bearing date at *York* the thirteenth of *June* 1642. with the Names of the Subſcribers. Two days after, his Majeſty in Council, taking notice of the Rumors ſpread, and Informations, given, which might induce many to believe, that his Majeſty intended to make War againſt his Parliament, " profeſſed before God, and
" ſaid, he declared to all the World, that he always
" had, and did abhor all ſuch Deſigns, and deſired
" all his Nobility and Council, who were there
" upon the place, to declare, whether they had not
" been witneſſes of his frequent and earneſt Declara-
" tions and Profeſſions to that purpoſe: Whether
" they ſaw any Color of Preparations or Counſels,
" that might reaſonably beget a belief of any ſuch
" Deſign; and whether they were not fully perſuad-
" ed, that his Majeſty had no ſuch Intention: But
" that all his Endeavours, according to his many
" Profeſſions, tended to the firm and conſtant Settle-
" ment of the true Proteſtant Religion; the juſt Pri-
" vileges of Parliament; the Liberty of the Subject;
" the Law, Peace, and Proſperity of this Kingdom:

BOOK V.

His Majeſty's Declaration and prohibition of June 15. 1642. diſavowing any Intention of raiſing War.

BOOK V.

The Declaration and profession of the Lords and Counsellors to the same effect.

Whereupon all the Lords, and Counsellors present, unanimously agreed, and did sign a Paper in these words:

"We, whose Names are underwritten, in Obedience to his Majesty's desire, and out of the Duty which we owe to his Majesty's Honor, and to Truth, being here upon the place, and Witnesses of his Majesty's frequent, and earnest Declarations and Professions of his abhorring all Designs of making War upon his Parliament; and not seeing any color of Preparations or Counsels, that might reasonably beget the belief of any such Designs, do profess before God, and testify to all the World, that we are fully persuaded that his Majesty hath no such intention: But that all his Endeavours tend to the firm and constant settlement of the true Protestant Religion; the just Privileges of Parliament; the Liberty of the Subject; the Law, Peace and Prosperity of this Kingdom. Which Testimony, and Declaration was Subscribed by

Lord *Littleton* Lord Keeper.	Duke of *Richmond*.	Earl of *Lindsey*.
Marquis of *Hertford*.	Earl of *Cumberland*.	Earl of *Bath*.
Earl of *Southampton*.	Earl of *Salisbury*.	Earl of *Dorset*.
Earl of *Devonshire*.	Earl of *Cambridge*.	Earl of *Northampton*.
Earl of *Clare*.	Earl of *Westmoreland*.	Earl of *Bristol*.
Earl of *Monmouth*.	Earl of *Rivers*.	Earl of *Berkshire*.
Earl of *Carnarvon*.	Earl of *Newport*.	Earl of *Dover*.
Lord *Willoughby* of *Eresby*.	Lord *Grey* of *Ruthin*.	Lord *Mowbray*, and *Martravers*.
Lord *Newark*.	Lord *Pawlet*.	Lord *Howard* of *Charleton*.
Lord *Rich*.	Lord *Savil*.	Lord *Lovelace*.
Lord *Coventry*.	Lord *Dunsmore*.	Lord *Mohun*.
Lord *Capel*.		Lord *Seymour*.
Lord *Falkland*.	Sir *P. Wich* Controller.	Secretary *Nicholas*.
	Sir *J. Colepepper* Chan. Exch.	Lord Chief Justice *Banks*.

This

This Testimony of the Lords and Counsellors was immediately printed, and published, together with a Declaration of his Majesty's, in which he said,

BOOK V.

"That though he had, in the last seven Months, met with so many several encounters of strange and unusual Declarations, under the Name of both his Houses of Parliament, that he shou'd not be amazed at any new Prodigy of that kind; and though their last of the 26:h of *May* gave him a fair warning that, the Contrivers of it having spent all their stock of bitter and reproachful Language upon him, he was now to expect they should break out into some bold, and disloyal Actions against him: And, having by that Declaration, as far in them lay, divested his Majesty of that Pe-eminence and Authority, which God, the Law, the Custom and Consent of this Nation had placed in him, and assumed it to Themselves, that they should likewise, with expedition, put forth the fruits of that Supreme Power, for the violating, and suppressing the other which they despised (an effect of which resolution, he said, their Declaration against his Proclamation concerning the pretended Ordinance for the Militia, and their punishing of the Proclaimers appeared to be) yet, he must confess, in their last Attempt (he said, he spoke of the last he knew; they might probably since, or at that present, have outdone That too) they had outdone what his Majesty had conceived was their present intention. And whosoever heard of Propositions, and Orders, for the bringing in Money or Plate to maintain

His Majesty's Declaration thereupon.

BOOK V.
"Horse, and Horsemen, and Arms, for the preservation of the Public Peace, or for the Defence of the King and both Houses of Parliament (such was their Declaration, or what they please to call it, of the tenth of *June*) would surely believe the Peace of the Kingdom to be extremely shaken; and, at least, the King himself to be consulted with, and privy to those Propositions. But, he said, he hoped, that when his good Subjects should find, that that goodly Pretence of defending the King, was but a specious bait to seduce weak, and inconsiderate Men into the highest Acts of disobedience and disloyalty against his Majesty, and of violence and destruction upon the Laws and Constitutions of the Kingdom, they would no longer be captivated by an implicit reverence to the Name of both Houses of Parliament; but would carefully examine, and consider what Number of Persons were present; and What persons were prevalent in those Consultations; and how the Debates were probably managed, from whence such horrid and monstrous Conclusions did result; and would at least weigh the Reputation, Wisdom, and affection of those, who were notoriously known out of the very horror of their Proceedings to have withdrawn themselves; or, by their skill and violence to be driven from Them, and their Counsels.

"His Majesty said, whilst their Fears and Jealousies did arise, or were infused into the People, from discourses of the Rebels in *Ireland*, of Skippers at *Rotterdam*, of Forces from *Denmark*, *France*,

"or *Spain* (how improbable and ridiculous soever
"that bundle of Information appeared to all wise,
"and knowing Men) it was no wonder if the easi-
"ness to deceive, and the willingness to be deceived,
"did prevail over many of his weak Subjects to
"believe, that the dangers, which they did not see,
"might proceed from causes which they did not
"understand: But for them to declare to all the
"world, that his Majesty intended to make War
"against his Parliament (whilst he sat still complain-
"ing to God Almighty of the injury offered to
"Him, and to the very Being of Parliaments) and
"that he had already begun actually to levy Forces
"both of Horse and Foot (whilst he had only, in a
"legal way, provided a smaller Guard for the secu-
"rity of his own Person so near a Rebellion at *Hull*,
"than They had, without Lawful Authority, above
"these eight Months, upon imaginary and impos-
"sible dangers) to impose upon his People's Sense,
"as well as their Understanding, by telling them
"his Majesty was doing that which they saw he was
"not doing, and intending that, they all knew, as
"much as Intentions could be known, he was not
"intending, was a boldness agreeable to no power
"but the Omnipotency of those Votes, whose ab-
"solute Supremacy had almost brought confusion
"upon the King and People; and against which
"no knowledge in matter of Fact, or Consent and
"Authority in matter of Law, they would endure
"should be opposed.

"His Majesty said, he had, upon all occasions,
"with all possible expressions, professed his firm and

"unshaken resolutions for Peace. And, he said, he did again, in the presence of Almighty God, his Maker and Redeemer, assure the world, that he had no more thought of making War against his Parliament, than against his own Children: That he would observe, and maintain the Acts assented to by him this Parliament without violation; of which, That for the frequent Assembling of Parliaments was one: And that he had not, nor would have, any thought of using any Force; unless he should be driven to it, for the security of his Person, and for the defence of the Religion, Laws, and Liberty of the Kingdom, and the just Rights and Privileges of Parliament: And therefore he hoped the Malignant Party, who had so much despised his Person, and usurped his Office, should not, by their specious fraudulent insinuations, prevail with his good Subjects to give credit to their wicked Assertions; and so to contribute their Power, and Assistance for the ruin and destruction of Themselves, and his Majesty.

"For the Guard about his Person (which, he said, not so much their Example, as their Provocation had enforced him to take) it was known it consisted of the prime Gentry, in fortune and reputation, of that Country, and of One Regiment of Trainedbands; who had been so far from offering any Affronts, Injuries, or Disturbance to any of his good Subjects, that their principal End was to prevent such; and so, might be Security, could be no Grievance to his People. That some ill affected Persons, or any Persons, had been employed in

"other parts to raise Troops, under color of his Ma-
"jesty's Service; or that such had made large, or any,
"offers of reward, and preferment to such as would
"come in, which had been alledged by them, was,
"he said, for ought he knew, or believed, an
"untruth devised by the Contrivers of that false
"Rumor. His Majesty disavowed it, and said he was
"confident there would be no need of any such Art,
"or Industry, to induce his loving Subjects, when
"they should see his Majesty oppressed, and their
"Liberties and Laws confounded (and till Then he
"would not call on them) to come in to him, and
"to assist him.

"For the Delinquents, whom his Majesty was said
"with a high and forcible hand to protect, he wished
"they might be named, and their Delinquency:
"And if his Majesty gave not satisfaction to Justice,
"when he should have received satisfaction concer-
"ning Sir *John Hotham* by his Legal Trial, Then
"let him be blamed. But if the design were, as
"it was well known to be, after his Majesty had
"been driven by force from his City of *London*,
"and kept by force from his Town of *Hull*, to pro-
"tect all those who were Delinquents against him,
"and to make all those Delinquents who attended
"on him, or executed his Lawful Commands, he
"said, he had great reason to be satisfied in the truth
"and justice of such Accusation, left to be his Ma-
"jesty's Servant, and to be a Delinquent, grew to
"Terms so convertible, that, in a short time, he
"were left as naked in Attendance, as they would
"have him in Power; and so compel him to be

"waited upon only by such whom They should
"appoint, and allow; and in whose presence he
"should be more miserably alone, than in desola-
"tion itself. And if the seditious Contrivers and
"Fomenters of that Scandal upon his Majesty, should
"have, as they had had, the power to mislead
"the Major part present of either or both Houses
"to make such Orders, and send such Messages and
"Messengers, as they had lately done, for the appre-
"hension of the great Earls and Barons of *England*, as
"if they were Rogues or Felons; and whereby
"Persons of Honor and Quality were made Delin-
"quents, merely for attending upon his Majesty
"and upon his Summons; whilst other Men were
"forbid to come near him, though obliged by the
"duty of their Place and Oaths, upon his Law-
"ful Commands: It was no wonder if Such Mes-
"sengers were not very well treated; and Such
"Orders not well obeyed; neither could there be a
"surer, or a cunninger way found out to render the
"Authority of both Houses scorned and vilified,
"than to assume to themselves (merely upon the
"Authority of the Name of Parliament) a Power
"monstrous to all understandings; and to do Ac-
"tions, and to make Orders, evidently and demon-
"strably contrary to all known Law, and Reason,
"(as to take up Arms against his Majesty under
"color of defending him; to cause Money to be
"brought in to Them, and to forbid his own Money
"to be paid to his Majesty, or to his use, under
"color that he would employ it ill; to beat him,
"and starve him for his own Good, and by his

"Power and Authority) which would in short time
"make the greatest Court, and greatest Person,
"cheap and of no estimation.

"Who those sensible Men were of the public
"Calamities, of the violations of the Privileges of
"Parliament, and the Common Liberty of the
"Subject, who had been baffled, and injured by
"Malignant Men, and Cavaliers about his Majesty,
"his Majesty said, he could not imagine. And if
"those Cavaliers were so much without the fear of
"God and Man, and so ready to commit all manner
"of outrage and violence, as was pretended, his
"Majesty's Government ought to be the more
"esteemed, which had kept them from doing so;
"insomuch as he believed, no Person had cause to
"complain of any injury, or of any damage, in the
"least degree, by any Man about his Majesty, or
"who had offered his Service to him. All which
"being, he said, duly considered, if the Contri-
"vers of those Propositions and Orders had been
"truly sensible of the obligations, which lay upon
"them in Honor, Conscience, and Duty, accord-
"ing to the high Trust reposed in them by his
"Majesty, and his People, they would not have
"published such a sense and apprehension of Immi-
"nent danger, when themselves, in their Con-
"sciences, knew that the greatest, and indeed only
"danger, which threatened the Church and State,
"the blessed Religion and Liberty of his People,
"was in their own desperate and seditious Designs;
"and would not have endeavoured, upon such weak
"and groundless reasons, to seduce his good Sub-

"jects from their Affection and Loyalty to him, to
"run themselves into Actions unwarrantable, and
"destructive to the Peace and Foundation of the
"Common-wealth.

"And that all his loving Subjects might see, how
"causeless and groundless that scandalous Rumor,
"and Imputation of his Majesty's raising War upon
"his Parliament, was, he had, with that his Decla-
"ration, caused to be printed the Testimony of
"those Lords, and other Persons of his Council,
"who were there with him; who, being upon the
"place, could not but discover such his Intentions
"and Preparations; and could not be suspected for
"their Honors and Interests to combine in such mis-
"chievous, and horrid resolutions.

"And therefore, his Majesty said, he straitly
"charged and commanded all his loving Subjects,
"upon their Allegiance, and as they would Answer
"the contrary at their Perils, that they should yield
"no obedience, or consent to the said Propositions
"and Orders; and that they presume not under any
"such Pretences, or by color of any such Orders,
"to raise or levy any Horse or Men, or to bring in
"any Money or Plate to such purpose. But, he
"said, if notwithstanding that clear Declaration,
"and Evidence of his intentions, those Men (whose
"design it was to compel his Majesty to raise War
"upon his Parliament; which all their skill and
"malice should never be able to effect) should think
"fit, by those Alarms, to awaken him to a more
"necessary care of the defence of Himself, and his
"People; and should Themselves, under color

" of Defence, in so unheard of a manner provide
" (and seduce others to do so too) to Offend his
" Majesty, having given him so lively a Testimony
" of their Affections, what they were willing to do,
" when they should once have made themselves
" Able; all his good Subjects would think it neces-
" sary for his Majesty to look to Himself. And he
" did therefore excite all his well affected People,
" according to their Oaths of Allegiance, and Su-
" premacy, and according to their solemn Vow,
" and Protestation (whereby they were obliged to
" defend his Person, Honor, and Estate) to con-
" tribute their best Assistance to the Preparations
" necessary for the opposing, and suppressing of the
" Trayterous Attempts of such wicked and ma-
" lignant Persons; who would destroy his Person,
" Honor, and Estate, and engage the whole King-
" dom in a Civil War, to satisfy their own lawless
" Fury and Ambition; and so rob his good Subjects
" of the blessed fruit of this present Parliament;
" which they already in some degree had, and might
" still reap, to the abundant satisfaction and joy of
" the whole Kingdom, if such wicked hands were
" not ready to ruin all their possessions, and frustrate
" all their hopes. And, in that case, his Majesty
" declared, that whosoever, of what Degree or
" Quality soever, should then, upon so urgent and
" visible necessity of His, and such apparent distrac-
" tion of the Kingdom, caused, and begotten by
" the malice and contrivance of that Malignant
" Party, bring in to his Majesty, and to his use,
" ready Money, or Plate; or should underwrite

"to furnish any Number of Horse, Horsemen, and
"Arms, for the preservation of the Public Peace
"and defence of his Person, and the vindication
"of the Privilege and Freedom of Parliament, he
"would receive it as a most acceptable Service,
"and as a Testimony of his singular Affection to
"the Protestant Religion, the Laws, Liberties,
"and Peace of the Kingdom; and would no longer
"desire the continuance of that Affection, than he
"would be ready to justify, and maintain the other
"with the hazard of his life."

And so concluded with the same Overtures They had done, in their Propositions for the Loan of Money at interest; "offering, for the security there-
"of, an Assurance of such his Lands, Forests,
"Parks, and Houses, as should be sufficient for
"the same; a more real security, he said, than the
"Name of public Faith, given without him, and
"against him; as if his Majesty were not part of the
"Public; And besides, he would always look upon
"it as a service most affectionately, and seasonably
"performed for the preservation of his Majesty,
"and the Kingdom. But, he said, he should be
"much gladder that their submission to those his
"Commands, and their desisting from any such
"Attempt of raising Horse or Men, might ease
"all his good Subjects of that charge, trouble,
"and vexation."

It will be wondered at hereafter, when, by what hath been said, the Number and Quality of the Peers is considered, who, by absenting themselves from the House, and their resort to his Majesty, sufficiently declared, that they liked not those Conclusions which begot those Distractions; why both those Peers and likewise such Members of the Commons, who then, and afterwards appeared in the King's Service, and were indeed full, or very near one Moiety of that House, did not rather, by their diligent and faithful Attendance in the Houses, according to their several Trusts reposed in them, discountenance and resist those pernicious and fatal transactions, than, by withdrawing themselves from their proper Stations, leave the other (whose ruinous Intentions were sufficiently discovered) possessed of the Reputation, Authority, and Power of a Parliament; by which, it was evident, the People would be easily, to a great degree, seduced. And though the observing Reader may, upon the collection of the several passages here set down, be able to answer those objections to himself; I am the rather induced, in this place, to apply myself to the clearing that Point, because not only many honest Men, who, at a distance, have considered it, without being Privy to the passages within the walls, and those breaches which fatally destroyed, and took away the Liberty and Freedom of those Councils, have been really troubled or unsatisfied with that Desertion, as they call it, of the Service to which they were incumbent, and chosen; but that I have heard some, who were the chief, if not the sole Promoters of those Violations, and the most violent Designs, and have since (out of the Ruptures, which have proceeded from their own Animosities) either been, or been thought to be, more

BOOK V.

moderately inclined, complain, "that the withdrawing of so many Members from the two Houses, was the Principal Cause of all Calamities." And they who have been the true Authors of them, and still continue the same men, have taken pains to make, and declare the others "Deserters of their Country, and betrayers of their Trusts, by their Voluntary withdrawing themselves from that Council."

In the doing whereof, I shall not, I cannot, make any excuse for those (of whom somewhat is before spoken) who, from the beginning of this Parliament, and in the whole progress of it, either out of laziness, or negligence, or incogitancy, or weariness, forbore to give their attendance there, when the Number of those who really intended these prodigious Alterations was very inconsiderable; and daily drew many to 'their opinions, upon no other ground than that the Number of the Dissenters appeared not equally diligent, and intent upon their Assertions: Neither can I excuse the Peers, the moderate Part whereof being Four for One, suffered themselves to be cozened, and persuaded, and threatened out of their Rights by a handful of Men, whom they might, in the beginning, easily have crushed; whereas in the House of Commons the great Managers were Men of notable parts, much reputation, admirable dexterity; Pretenders to severe justice, and regularity; and then the Number of the weak, and the wilful, who naturally were to be guided by them, always made up a Major part; so that, from the beginning, they were always

OF THE REBELLION.

able to carry whatsoever they set their hearts visibly upon; at least, to discredit, or disgrace any particular Man against whom they thought necessary to proceed, albeit of the most unblemished reputation, and upon the most frivolous suggestions; so that they could not but be very formidable, in that House, to all but the most abstracted Men from all vulgar considerations.

But, I am confident, whosoever diligently revolves the several passages in both Houses, from the time of the publishing the first Remonstrance, upon his Majesty's Return from *Scotland*, to the time of which we last speak, must be of opinion, that the resorting of so many Members Then to his Majesty (from whom all the Lords, and some of the Commons, received Commands to that purpose) or to such places, where they thought they might be of greatest use to his Majesty in preservation of the Peace of the Kingdom, was not only an Act of Duty, but of such Prudence and Discretion, as sober and honest Men were to be guided by. In the House of Peers, the Bishops, who had as much Right to sit there, and were as much Members of Parliament as any Lord there, were first, by direct violence and force, a great part of them, driven and kept from thence, till the Bill, for the Total expulsion of the whole Order from those seats, was passed; such of the Peers, who were most remarkable for adhering to the Government of the Church, being, in the mean time, threatened publicly by the Rabble; and some of their Persons Assaulted. The business of the Militia had been twice, upon solemn debate in a full House, rejected there; till such force and violence was brought to the very doors, such expostulations and threats delivered within the doors against those who refused to concur with them in that business, that no Man had reason to believe his life out of danger from those rude hands, who was taken notice of for an Opposer of their unreasonable desires; some of them having been declared Enemies to their Country, for having refused what was in their power lawfully to refuse; and others having been Criminally accused by the Commons, for Words spoken by them in Debates of the House of Peers; after which many of them were sent for, by special Letters, to attend his Majesty (which Letters were always thought to be a good, and warrantable, and sufficient ground to be absent from the House; nor had such Summons, from the beginning of Parliaments to this present, ever been neglected) with whom they had not been many weeks, but two of them, as hath been mentioned before, upon an untrue and extravagant information, without further examination, were declared Enemies to the Kingdom; and nine others by solemn judgment, upon an Impeachment brought up by the Commons against them, only for being absent, and for what only concerned the Privilege and Jurisdiction of the Peers, were disabled to sit in the House again during this Session; so that, if they would have returned, they were actually excluded that Council.

In the House of Commons, the case was worse: First, they who had, with that Liberty which is essential to Parliaments, and according to their understandings, dissented or declared a dislike of what the Violent Party so vehemently pursued, were, as hath been said before, declared Enemies to their Country; and their Names posted up in Paper, or Parchment, at most eminent places, under some opprobrious Character; which, though it was not avowed, and had no Authority from the House by any public Act, yet, being complained of, was neither redressed, nor was the complaint so countenanced, that it could be concluded the Violation was unacceptable: so, though the Tumults were not directly summoned or assembled, it is evident, by what hath been before set forth truly and at large, that they found there visible countenance, and encouragement.

Then, what had been, upon full and solemn Debates in a full House, rejected, was many times, in a thin House, and at unusual and unparliamentary Hours, resumed, and determined contrary to the former Conclusions: Yet Men satisfied themselves with doing what they thought their Duty, and reasonably opposing what the Major part ordered to be done; hoping that Men's understandings would be shortly better informed; and that though high and irreverent Expressions, and Words were sometimes used against the King, there would be abstaining from unlawful and dangerous Actions; and that the House of Peers, at least, would never be brought to join, or concur in any Act prejudicial to the Sovereign power. But when they saw a new way found out by the dexterity of the Major part in the House of Commons, to make the Minor part of

BOOK V.

the Lords too hard for the Major; and so, whilst all Men were transported with jealousy of the breach of Privilege of Parliament by the King, that there was, by the Houses Themselves, an absolute rooting up of all Privileges: That from Metaphysical considerations, what *might* be done in case of necessity, the Militia of the Kingdom was Actually seized on; and put under a Command contrary to, and against the King's Command: That there was then a Resolution taken, by those who could Act their Resolutions when they pleased, to make a General, and to oblige all the Members to live and die with that General; which will be anon more particularly mentioned (for that Resolution was well known before the time that those many Members removed to *York*, and withdrew to other places; and was executed within three or four days after) Men thought it high time to look to their innocence, and (since by the Course and Orders of that House, they could leave no monument or evidence of their dissenting, as the Lords might, by their Protestations upon any unlawful Act, or Resolution) to declare their dislike of what was Done, by not being present at the Doing: And it was reasonably thought, there being no other way peaceably and securely to do it, that the Kingdom, understanding the Number of those that were present at such new transactions, and weighing the Quality, Number, and Reputation of those who were absent, would be best induced to prefer the old Laws of the Kingdom, before the new Votes (destructive to those Laws) of those few Men, who called themselves the two Houses

of

of Parliament; and that it would prove a good Expedient to work upon the consciences, and modesty of those who stayed behind, to conclude it necessary, by some fair Addresses to his Majesty, to endeavour such a general good understanding, that a perfect union might be made; and the Privilege, Dignity, and Security of Parliament, be established according to the true, and just Constitution of it.

It is true, how reasonably soever it might be expected, it produced not that Ingenuity; but they who had been troubled with the company of them that afterwards withdrew, and, by the opposition they made, could not make that expedition in the mischief they intended, were glad they were rid of them; yet, shortly, considering what influence indeed it might have upon understanding Men, they found a way to cast a reproach upon those who were absent, and yet to prevent any inconvenience to themselves by their return; publishing an Order, " that all the Members absent should appear at such " a day, under the Penalty of paying each 100 l. fine " for his absence;" and whosoever did not appear at that day (which gave not time enough to any who were at a distance) " should not presume to sit " in the House, before he had paid his fine, and " satisfied the House with the cause of his absence;" So that all those who were with the King, and very many more, who had really withdrawn themselves to refresh their minds, or upon necessary affairs of their own, with a purpose to return, clearly discerned themselves excluded from sitting any more there; it being sufficiently manifest, that the Cause of their absence would never be approved, if their Persons were disliked, and their Opinions disapproved: Which appeared quickly; for the day was no sooner past, but they, without the least warrant of Precedent or color of Right, expelled very many, sometimes twenty a day, not only of those who were with the King, but of others who had given them equal distaste; and ordered new Writs to issue out to chuse other Members in their Rooms.

It cannot be denied but some very honest and entire Men stayed still there, and opposed all their unjustifiable proceedings with great courage, and much liberty of Speech; which was more frankly permitted to them than had been before, when the Number of the Dissenters was greater; and it may be there are still some who satisfy themselves that they have performed their Duty, by always having denied to give their consent to whatsoever hath been seditiously, or illegally concluded. But I must Appeal to the consciences of those very Men, whether they have not been many times, by staying there, compelled, or terrified to do, and submit to many Acts contrary to their Conscience, in cases of Conscience; and contrary to their Judgment and Knowledge, in matters of Law, and Right; and contrary to their Oaths and Duties, in matters of Allegiance; and whether if they had refused so to do, they should not have been plundered, expelled, and committed to Prison? And then They cannot be thought to have proceeded unreasonably, who, to preserve their Innocence, and their Liberty, chose to undergo all the other Censures and Difficulties which could befalthem, and which have been since plentifully poured upon them But to return.

The King had at this time, called to him some Judges, and Lawyers of eminence; by whose Advice he published a Declaration concerning the Militia, and asserted "the Right of the Crown in granting "Commissions of Array, for the better ordering "and governing thereof;" and, at the same time, issued out those Commissions to all Counties, "ex- "pressly forbidding any obedience to be given to "the Ordinance for the Militia by both Houses, "under the penalty of High-Treason." This only improved the Paper-combate in Declarations; either Party insisting, "that the Law was on Their side;" and the People giving obedience to either, according to their conveniences: And many did believe, that if the King had resorted to the old known way of Lord Lieutenants, and Deputy Lieutenants, his service would have been better carried on; the Commission of Array being a thing they had not before heard of, though founded upon an Ancient Act of Parliament in the Reign of *Hen* iv. and so was received with jealousy, and easily discredited by the glosses and suggestions of the Houses

Besides that some Men of very good Affections to the Crown, and averse enough to the extravagant pretences and proceedings of the Parliament, did not conceal their prejudice to the Commission of Array, as not warranted by Law; which did very much work upon other Men, and made the obedience less cheerful that was given to that service. Mr. *Selden* had, in the Debate upon that Subject in the House of Commons, declared himself very positively, and with much sharpness against the Commission of Array, as a thing expresly without any Authority of Law; the Statute upon which it was grounded being, as he said, repealed; and discoursed very much of the ill Consequences, which might result from submitting to it: He answered the Arguments which had been used to support it; and easily prevailed with the House not to like a proceeding, which they knew was intended to do them hurt, and to lessen their Authority. But his Authority and Reputation prevailed much further than the House, and begot a prejudice against it in many well affected Men without doors: When the King was informed of it, he was much troubled, having looked upon Mr. *Selden* as well disposed to his Service. And the Lord *Falkland*, with his Majesty's leave, writ a friendly Letter to Mr. *Selden*, "to know his reason, "why, in such a conjuncture, whatever his opinion "were, he would oppose the submission to the Com- "mission of Array, which no body could deny "to have had it's original from Law, and which "many Learned Men still believed to be very Legal, "to make way for the establishment of an Ordi- "nance, which had no manner of pretence to Right." He Answered this Letter very frankly; as a Man who believed himself in the right upon the Commission of Array, and that the Arguments he had used against it could not be Answered; summing up some of those Arguments in as few words as they could be comprehended in: But then he did as frankly inveigh against the Ordinance for the Militia,

" which, he said, was without any shadow of Law
" or pretence of Precedent, and most destructive to
" the Government of the Kingdom: And he did
" acknowledge, that he had been the more inclined
" to make that discourse in the House against the
" Commission, that he might with the more free-
" dom argue against the Ordinance; which was to
" be considered upon a day then appointed: And
" was most confident, that he should likewise over-
" throw the Ordinance: which, he confessed, could
" be less supported, and he did believe, that it would
" be much better, if both were rejected, than if
" either of them should stand, and remain uncon-
" trolled." But his confidence deceived him; and
he quickly found, that They who suffered themselves to be entirely governed by his Reason, when
those Conclusions resulted from it which contributed to their own designs, would not be at all
guided by it, or submit to it, when it persuaded that
which contradicted, and would disappoint those
designs: And so, upon the day appointed for the
debate of their Ordinance, when he applied all his
faculties to the convincing them of the illegality and
monstrousness of it, by arguments at least as clear
and demonstrable as his former had been, they made
no impression upon them; but were easily answered
by those who with most Passion insisted upon their
own sense. He had satisfied them very well, when
he concurred with them in judgment; but his Reasons were weak, when they crossed their Resolutions. So most Men are deceived in being too reasonable; concluding that Reason will prevail upon

BOOK V.

those Men to submit to what is Right and Just, who have no other consideration of Right or Justice, but as it advances their Interest, or complies with their Humor, and Passion. And so easy it hath always been to do harm, and to mislead Men, and so hard to do good, and reduce them to Reason.

The Parliament's Declaration to the City, upon a Letter from the King to the L. Mayor, and Aldermen.

These Paper-skirmishes left neither side better inclined to the other; but, by sharpening each other, drew the matter nearer to an issue. The King had written a Letter to the Mayor and Aldermen of *London*, and to the Masters and Wardens of each Company; by which, "he assured them, of his de-
" sire of the Peace of the Kingdom; and therefore re-
" quired them, as they tendered their Charter of
" the City, and their own particular Welfares, not
" to bring in Horses, Money, or Plate, upon the
" Propositions of the Houses, whereby, under pre-
" tence of raising a Guard for the Parliament, For-
" ces would be levied, and, in truth, employed
" against his Majesty:" Of which the Houses taking notice, published a Declaration to the City, "That
" they could not be secured by his Majesty's Pro-
" testations, that his desires, and purposes were for
" the Public Peace; since it appeared, by divers ex-
" pressions, and proceedings of his Majesty, that
" he intended to use Force against those who sub-
" mitted to the Ordinance of the Militia; and that
" he had likewise some intention of making an At-
" tempt upon *Hull*. In both which cases, they did
" declare, that whatsoever Violence should be used,
" either against those who exercise the Militia, or
" against *Hull*, They could not but believe it as

"done against the Parliament. They told them that
"the dangerous, and mischievous intentions of
"some about his Majesty were such, that what-
"soever was most precious to Men of Conscience
"and Honor, as Religion, Liberty, and Public
"Safety, were like to be overwhelmed and lost in
"the general confusion and calamity of the King-
"dom; which would not only question, but over-
"throw the Charter of the City of *London*; expose
"the Citizens, their Wives and Children, to vio-
"lence and villany; and leave the Wealth of that
"famous City as a Prey to those desperate, and
"necessitous Persons: And therefore they forbid
"all the Officers to publish that Paper, as they
"would answer their Contempt to the Parliament,
"by the Power and Authority of which, they
"assured them, they should be protected, and se-
"cured in their Persons, Liberties, and Estates, for
"whatsoever they should do by Their advice or
"persuasion.

To this the King replied, "That he wondered
"since they had usurped the supreme Power to
"themselves, they had not taken upon them the
"supreme Style too; and directed their very new
"Declaration to their Trusty and Well-beloved,
"their Subjects of the City of *London* : For it was
"too great and palpable a Scorn, to persuade them
"to take up Arms against his Persons, under Color
"of being loving Subjects to his Office; and to de-
"stroy his Person, that they might preserve the
"King: That he was beholding to them, that they
"had explained to all his good Subjects the meaning

BOOK V.

The King's Reply.

BOOK V.

"of their Charge against his Majesty, that by his intention of making War against his Parliament, no more was pretended to be meant, but his resolution not to submit to the high Injustice and Indignity of the Ordinance for the Militia, and the business of *Hull*. He said, he had never concealed his intentions in either of those Particulars (he wished They would deal as clearly with Him) but had always, and did now declare, That that pretended Ordinance was against the Law of the Land; against the Liberty and Property of the Subject; destructive to Sovereignty; and therefore not consistent with the very Constitution and Essence of the Kingdom, and the Right and Privilege of Parliament: That he was bound by his Oath (and all his Subjects were bound by theirs of Allegiance, and Supremacy, and their own Protestation lately taken, to assist his Majesty) to oppose that Ordinance, which was put already in execution against him, not only by Training and Arming his Subjects, but by forcibly removing the Magazine, from the place trusted by the County, to their own Houses, and guarding it there with Armed Men: Whither it would be next removed, and how used by such Persons, he knew not.

"That the keeping his Majesty out of *Hull* by Sir *John Hotham*, was an Act of High-Treason against his Majesty; and the taking away his Magazine and Munition from him, was an Act of Violence upon his Majesty, by what hands or by whose direction soever it was done: And, in both

" cases, by the help of God, and the Law, his
" Majesty said, he would have Justice, or lose his
" Life in the requiring it; the which he did not
" value at that rate, as to preserve it with the In-
" famy of suffering himself to be robbed, and spoiled
" of that Dignity he was born to. And if it were
" possible for his good Subjects to believe, that
" such a Defence of himself, with the utmost power
" and strength he could raise, was making a War
" against his Parliament, he did not doubt, however
" it should please God to dispose of him in that con-
" tention, but the justice of his Cause would, at
" the last, prevail against those few Malignant
" Spirits, who, for their own ends and ambitious
" designs, had so misled and corrupted the under-
" standings of his People. And since neither his own
" Declaration, nor the Testimony of so many of his
" Lords, then with his Majesty, could procure cre-
" dit with those Men, but that they proceeded to
" levy Horse, and to raise Money and Arms against
" his Majesty, he said, he was not to be blamed,
" if after so many gracious expostulations with them
" upon undeniable principles of Law and Reason
" (which they answered only by Voting that which
" his Majesty said, to be neither Law, nor Reason;
" and so proceeded actually to levy War upon his
" Majesty, to justify that which could not be other-
" wise defended) at last he made such provision,
" that as he had been driven from *London*, and kept
" from *Hull*, he might not be surprised at *York*; but
" be in a condition to resist, and bring to justice
" those Men, who would persuade his People that

"their Religion was in danger, becaufe his Majefty would not confent it fhould be in Their power to alter it by their Votes; or their Liberty in danger, becaufe he would allow no Judge of that Liberty, but the known Law of the Land: Yet, he faid, whatever provifion he fhould be compelled to make for his fecurity, he would be ready to lay down, as foon as they fhould revoke the Orders by which they had made Levies, and fubmitted thofe Perfons, who had detained his Towns, carried away his Arms, and put the Militia in execution contrary to his Proclamation, to that Trial of their innocence, which the Law had directed, and to which they were born: If that were not fubmitted to, he fhould, with a good confcience, proceed againft thofe who fhould prefume to exercife that pretended Ordinance for the Militia, and the other who fhould keep his Town of *Hull* from him, as he would refift Perfons who came to take away his Life, or his Crown from him.

" And therefore his Majefty again remembered, and required his City of *London* to obey his former Commands, and not to be mifled by the Oration of thofe Men, who were made defperate by their Fortunes, or their Fortunes by Them; who told them their Religion, Liberty, and Property, was to be preferved no other way, but by their Difloyalty to his Majefty: That they were now at the brink of the River, and might draw their Swords (which was an expreffion ufed at a great convention of the City) when nothing purfued them but

" their own evil consciences. He wished them to
" consider, whether their Estates came to them,
" and were settled upon them, by Orders of both
" Houses, or by that Law which his Majesty defen-
" ded: What security they could have to enjoy
" their own, when they had helped to rob his Ma-
" jesty; and what a happy conclusion That War
" was like to have, which was raised to oppress
" their Sovereign: That the wealth and glory of
" their City was not like to be destroyed any other
" way, but by Rebelling against his Majesty; and
" that way inevitably it must; nor their Wives and
" Children to be exposed to violence and villany,
" but by those who make their Appetite and Will
" the measure, and guide to all their Actions. He
" advised them not to fancy to themselves Melan-
" choly apprehensions, which were capable of no
" satisfaction; but seriously to consider what security
" they could have, that they had not under his Ma-
" jesty, or had not been offered by him: And whe-
" ther the Doctrine those Men taught, and would
" have them defend, did not destroy the Founda-
" tions upon which their security was built?

The great conflux that hath been mentioned, of Men of all Conditions, and Qualities, and Humors, could not continue long together at *York*, without some impatience and commotion; and most Men wondered, that there appeared no provisions to be made towards a War, which they saw would be, inevitable: And when the Levies of Soldiers under the Earl of *Essex* were hastened with so much vigor, that the King should have no other Preparations towards an Army, than a single Troop of Guards made up of Gentlemen Volunteers; who, all Men foresaw, would quit the Troop when there should be an Army: And many do yet believe, that the King too long deferred his recourse to Arms; and that if he had raised Forces upon his first repulse at *Hull*, his service would have been very much advanced; and that the Parliament would not have been able to have drawn an Army together. And so Men still reproach the Councils which were then about the King, as they were censured by many at that time; but neither They then, nor These now do understand the true reason thereof. The King had not, at that time, one Barrel of Powder, nor one Musquet, nor any other provision necessary for an Army; and, which was worse, was not sure of any Port, to which they might be securely assigned; nor had he Money for the support of his own Table for the term of one Month. He expected, with impatience, the arrival of all those necessaries, by the care and activity of the Queen; who was then in *Holland*, and by the sale of her own, as well as of the Crown-Jewels, and by the friendship of *Henry* Prince of *Orange*, did all she could to provide all that was necessary; and the King had newly directed her to send all to *New-Castle*, which was but then secured to him by the diligence of the Earl of that Name. In the mean time both the King Himself, and they who best knew the state of his Affairs, seemed to be without any thoughts of making War; and to hope, that the Parliament would at last incline to some Accommodation; for which both his Majesty, and those Persons were exposed to a thousand reproaches.

The Queen had many difficulties to contend with; for though the Prince of *Orange* had a very signal affection for the King's Service, and did all he could to dispose the States to concern themselves in his Majesty's Quarrel; yet his Authority, and Interest, was much diminished with the vigor of his Body and Mind: And the States of *Holland* were so far from being inclined to the King, that they did him all the mischief they could. They had before assisted the Rebellion in *Scotland*, with giving them credit for Arms and Ammunition, before they had money to buy any; and they did afterwards, several ways, discover their affections to the Parliament; which had so many Spies there, that the Queen could do nothing they had not present notice of; so that it was no easy matter for the Queen to provide Arms and Ammunition, but the Parliament had present notice of it, and of the ways which were thought upon to transport them to the King: And then their Fleet, under the Command of the Earl of *Warwick*, lay ready to obstruct and intercept that Communication; nor was any remedy in view to remove this mischief; insomuch as it was no easy thing for the King to send to, or to receive Letters from, the Queen.

There was a small Ship of 28 or 30 Guns, that was part of the Fleet that wafted her Majesty into *Holland* from *Dover*, which was called the Providence, under the Command of Captain *Straugham*, when the Fleet was Commanded by Sir *John*

Pennington, and before the Earl of *Warwick* was superinduced into that Charge against the King's Will. That Ship, the Captain whereof was known to be faithful to his Majesty, was, by the Queen, detained and kept in *Holland* from the time of her Majesty's Arrival, under several pretences, of which the Captain made use, when he afterwards received Orders from the Earl of *Warwick* " to repair to the " Fleet in the *Downs*;" until, after many promises and excuses, it was at last discerned that he had other Business and Commands; and so was watched, by the other Ships, as an enemy. This Vessel the Queen resolved to send to the King, principally to inform his Majesty of the straits she was in; of the provisions she had made; and to return with such particular Advice, and Directions from his Majesty, that she might take further resolutions: And because the Vessel was light, and drew not much Water, and so could run into any Creek, or open Road, or Harbour, and, from thence, easily send an express to the King; there was put into it about two hundred Barrels of Powder, and two or three thousand Arms with seven or eight Field-Pieces; which, they knew, would be very welcome to the King, and serve for a beginning and countenance to draw Forces together. The Captain was no sooner put to Sea, but notice was sent to the Commander of the Fleet in the *Downs*; who immediately sent three or four Ships to the North, which easily got the Providence in View, before it could reach that Coast; and chased it with all their Sails, till they saw it enter into the River of *Humber*;

OF THE REBELLION.

when, looking upon it as their own, they made less haste to follow it, being content to drive it before them into their own Port of *Hull*; there being, as they thought, no other way to escape them; until they plainly saw the Ship entering into a narrow Creek out of *Humber*, which declined *Hull*, and led into the Country some Miles above it; which was a place well known to the Captain, and designed by him to arrive at from the beginning. It was in vain for them to hasten their pursuit; for they quickly found that their great Ships could not enter into that passage, and that the River was too shallow to follow him; and, so, with shame and anger, they gave over the Chase; whilst the Captain continued his course; and having never thought of saving the Ship, run it on Shore on that side towards *Burlington*; and, with all expedition, gave notice to the King of his arrival; who, immediately, caused the Persons of Quality, in the parts adjacent, to draw the Trained-bands of the Country together, to secure the incursions from *Hull*; and by this means, the Arms, Ammunition, and Artillery, were quickly brought to *York*.

The King was well content that it should be generally believed, that this small Ship, the size whereof was known to few, had brought a greater quantity and proportion of Provisions for the War, than in truth it had; and therefore, though it had brought no Money, which he expected, he forthwith granted Commissions, to raise Regiments of Horse and Foot, to such Persons of Quality and Interest, as were able to comply with their obligations. He declared the Earl of *Lindsey*, Lord High Chamberlain of *England*, his General of the Army; a Person of great Honor and Courage, and generally beloved; who many years before had good Commands in *Holland*, and *Germany*, and had been Admiral at Sea in several Expeditions. Sir *Jacob Ashley* was declared Major General of the Foot, a Command he was very equal to, and had exercised before, and executed after, with great approbation. The Generalship of the Horse, his Majesty preserved for his Nephew Prince *Rupert*; who was daily expected, and arrived soon after: And all Levies were hastened with as much expedition as was possible in so great a scarcity, and notorious want of Money; of which no more need be said, after it is remembered that all the Lords, and Council about the King, with several other Persons of Quality, voluntarily made a Subscription for the payment of so many Horse for three Months; in which time they would needs believe, that the War should be at an end; every one paying down what the three Months pay would amount to, into the hands of a Treasurer appointed to receive it; and this Money was presently paid for the making those Levies of Horse, which were designed; and which could not have been made but by those Moneys.

And now the King thought it time to execute a Resolution he had long intended, and which many Men wondered he neglected so long; which was, as much as in him lay, to take the Admiralty into his own hands. He had long too much cause to be unsatisfied, and displeased with the Earl of *Northumberland*;

berland; whom he thought he had obliged above any Man whatsoever. His delivering the Fleet into the hands and Command of the Earl of *Warwick*, after his Majesty had expresly refused it to the Parliament, the King could not easily forgive; however he thought it not Then seasonable to resent it, because he had nothing to object against him, but his compliance with the Command of the Parliament, who would have owned it as their own quarrel; and must have obliged that Earl to put his whole Interest into Their hands, and to have run Their Fortune; to which he was naturally too much inclined: And then his Majesty foresaw, that there would have been no Fleet at all set out that year, by their having the Command of all the Money, which was to be applied to that Service. Whereas, by his Majesty's concealing his resentment, there was a good Fleet made ready, and set out; and many Gentlemen settled in the Command of Ships, of whose Affection and Fidelity his Majesty was assured, that no Superior Officer could corrupt it; but that they would, at all times, repair to their Service, whenever he required it. And, indeed, his Majesty had an opinion of the devotion of the whole body of the Common Sea-men to his Service, because he had, bountifully, so much mended their condition, and increased their Pay, that he thought they would have even thrown the Earl of *Warwick* over Board, when he should Command them; and so the respiting the doing of it would be of little importance. But now, that a Ship of his own, in the execution of his Commands, should be chased

BOOK V.

by his own Fleet as an Enemy, made such a noise in all places, even to his reproach and dishonor, that he could no longer defer the doing what he had so long thought of. He resolved therefore, to revoke the Earl of *Northumberland*'s Commission of the Office of High-Admiral of *England*, and to send the Revocation to him under the Great Seal of *England*: Then, to send Sir *John Pennington*, who was then at *York*, on board the Fleet, and to take the Charge of it: and Letters were prepared, and signed by the King, to every one of the Captains; whereby they were required, " to observe the " Orders of Sir *John Pennington*." And all this was carried with all possible Secrecy, that none, but those few who were trusted, knew, or suspected any such Alteration.

But the King thought fit, first to advise with Sir *John Pennington*; of whose Integrity he was confident, and whose judgment he always principally relied on in all his Maritime Actions; and thought him the only Person fit immediately to take the Fleet out of the Earl of *Warwick*'s possession; who had dispossessed Him the Command that year, which he had usually exercised. Sir *John Pennington*, finding the matter full of difficulty, and the execution like to meet with some interruptions, expressed no alacrity to undertake it in his own Person; alledging, " that himself stood in the Parliament's disfavor, " and jealousy (which was true) and that therefore " his motion, and journey toward the *Downs*, where " the Fleet then lay, would be immediately taken " notice of; and his Majesty's Design be so much

"guessed at, that there would need no other Disco-
" very;" but he propounded to his Majesty, "that
" he would send a Letter to Sir *Robert Manfel*, who
" lived at *Greenwich*, speedily to go to the Fleet,
" and to take charge of it, and that His Authority,
" being Vice-Admiral of *England*, and his known
" and great Reputation with the Sea-men, would
" be like to meet with the least resistance." His
Majesty, imparting this Counsel to those whom he
had made Privy to his purpose, entered upon new
considerations; and concluded, " that Sir *Robert*
" *Manfel*'s age (though his Courage and Integrity
" were unquestionable) and the accidents that de-
" pended upon that, would render that Expedient
" most hazardous; and that, in truth, there needed
" no such absolute and supreme Officer, to be ap-
" pointed in the first Article; but rather, that his
" Majesty should direct his special Letter to the
" Captain of every Ship, requiring him immediately
" to weigh Anchor, and to bring away his Ship to
" such a place as his Majesty might appoint, where
" he should receive further Orders: And to that
" place he might send such an Officer, as he thought
" fit to trust with the Command of the whole Navy
" so assembled." According to this Resolution, the
whole Despatch was prepared. First a Revocation
of the Earl of *Northumberland's* Commission of Admiral, under the Great Seal of *England*; of which
there was a Duplicate; the one to be sent to his Lordship; the other to the Earl of *Warwick*; whose Commission was founded upon, and so determined by,
the other. Then a particular Letter to each of the

Captains of his Ships, informing them "of his Majesty's Revocation of the Admiral's Patent, and, "consequently, of the determination of the Earl of "Warwick's Commission" (to whom his Majesty likewise writ, to "inhibit him from further meddling "in that Charge)" and therefore commanding them to yield no further obedience to either of their Orders; but that, immediately upon the receipt of those his Royal Letters, he should weigh Anchor; and with what speed he might, repair to *Burlington-Bay* upon the Coast of *Yorkshire*; where he should receive his Majesty's further pleasure: And so each Commander, without relation to any other Commands, had no more to look after but his own Ship, and his own Duty, by which the King might expect, at least, so many Ships as were under the Command of those who had any Affection or Fidelity to his Service.

Accordingly, all things being prepared, and signed by the King and sealed, what immediately concerned the Earl of *Northumberland* was delivered to one of his Majesty's Pages, to be given to the Earl of *Northumberland* at *London*; and the whole despatch to the Fleet to Mr. *Edward Villiers*, whose diligence and dexterity his Majesty found fit for any Trust; the former being directed "not to make such haste, "but that the other might be at least as soon at the "*Downs*, as He at *London*;" and Mr. *Villiers* again being appointed what Letters he should first deliver to the Captains; "and that he should Visit the Earl "of *Warwick* in the last place;" that his Activity might have no influence upon the Seamen to prevent their obedience to his Majesty. And surely if this resolution had been pursued, it is very probable, that the King had been Master of very many of his Ships again. But, when the Messengers were dispatched, and well instructed, and he that was for *London* gone on his Journey, there was a sudden and unexpected change of the whole direction to the Fleet, by Sir *John Pennington's* repair to his Majesty; and, upon second thoughts, offering " to go Himself to the *Downs*, and to take Charge of the Fleet;" which changed the Forms of the Letters to the several Captains; and, instead of leaving every one to use his best expedition to bring away his own Ship to *Burlington*, " required them only to observe such " Orders, as they should receive by Sir *John Pen-* " *nington*;" who thought not fit (for the reasons formerly given of his being taken notice of) to go with Mr. *Villiers*; but, by Him, writ to Sir *Henry Palmer*, to whom likewise his Majesty sent a Letter to that purpose, being an Officer of the Navy, and who lived by the *Downs*, " immediately to go aboard " the Admiral; and that he Himself would make " all possible haste to him, setting out at the same " time with Mr. *Villiers*; but Journeying a further " and more private way." Mr. *Villiers*, left, by his stay for the alteration of his despatches, the Page's coming to *London* sooner than was intended at his setting out, might produce some inconvenience to the service, slept not till he came to Sir *Henry Palmer*; who, being infirm in his health, and surprised with the Command, could not make that expedition aboard, as might have been requisite; though he was Loyally and Zealously affected to his Majesty's Service. However, Mr. *Villiers* hastened to the Ships which lay then at Anchor, and according to his Instructions, delivered his several Letters to the Captains; the greatest part whereof received them with great expressions of duty and submission, expecting only to receive Sir *John Pennington*'s Orders, for which they stayed; and, without doubt, if either the first Letters had been sent, or Sir *John Pennington* been present, when these others were delivered, his Majesty had been possessed of the greatest part of the Fleet; the Earl of *Warwick* being at that time, according to his usual Licences, with some Officers, whose company he liked, on shore making merry; so that there was only his Vice-Admiral, Captain *Batten*, on board; who was of eminent disaffection to his Majesty: The Rear-Admiral, Sir *John Mennes*, being of unquestionable Integrity.

But after five or six hours (in which time nothing could be acted, for want of advice and direction; enough being ready to Obey, but none having Authority to Command) the Earl of *Warwick* came aboard his Ship, to whom Mr. *Villiers* likewise gave his Majesty's Letters of his Discharge; who, without any Declaration of disobeying it, applied himself to the confirming those whom he thought true to his Party, and diligently to watch the rest; presuming, that he should speedily hear from those by whom he had been originally trusted.

In the mean time, the Captains expected Orders from Sir *John Pennington*; who likewise privately expected such an account from Sir *Henry Palmer*, as

might encourage him to come to the Ships. But this unfortunate delay disappointed all: For the other Gentleman, according to his Instructions, having reached *London* in the evening after the Houses were risen, delivered the King's Letter, and the Discharge of his Commission, to the Earl of *Northumberland*; who, with all shows of Duty and Submission, expressed "his resolution to obey his Majesty; and a "hearty sorrow, that he had, by any Misfortune, "incurred his Majesty's displeasure." How ingenuous soever this demeanour of his Lordship's was, the business was quickly known to those who were more concerned in it; who were exceedingly perplexed, with the apprehension of being dispossessed of so great a part of their strength, as the Royal Fleet; and earnestly pressed the Earl of *Northumberland*, " that, notwithstanding such his Majesty's Revoca-
" tion, he would still continue the execution of his
" Office of Lord High Admiral; in which they
" would assist him with their utmost and full Power,
" and Authority. But his Lordship alledging, that
" it would ill become Him, who had received that
" Charge from the King with so notable circumstan-
" ces of Trust and Favor, to continue the possession
" thereof against his express Pleasure, there being a
" Clause in his Grant, that it should be only during
" such time as his Majesty thought fit to use his
" Service;" and so, " utterly refusing to meddle
" further in it;" as soon as they could get the Houses together the next morning, they easily agreed to pass an Ordinance, as they call it, " to appoint the
" Earl of *Warwick* to be Admiral of that Fleet, with

The King revokes the Earl of Northumberland's Commission of Admiral.

"as full and ample Authority, as he had before had "from the Earl of *Northumberland.*" Which Ordinance, together with Letters, and Votes of encouragement to his Lordship and to the Officers and Seamen, they speedily sent, by a Member of their own; who arrived therewith, the next morning, after Mr. *Villiers* had delivered the King's Letters; Sir *John Pennington* in the mean time neither coming, nor sending any further Advice.

The Earl of *Warwick*, being thus armed, found himself Master of his Work; and immediately summoned all the Captains, to attend him on board his Ship in Council; the which all but two did (Captain *Slingsby*, and Captain *Wake*) who, being by his Majesty's Letters, as the rest were, expressly charged to yield no further obedience to the Earl of *Warwick*, refused to repair to him; making themselves ready to resist any violence, and putting their Ships in order to go out to Sea, that they might be at Liberty to attend his Majesty's Commands; but they were so encompassed by the whole Fleet, and the dexterity of the Earl's Ministers was such, and the devotion, generally, of the Sea-men so tainted, and corrupted from the King's Service, that, instead of carrying away the Ships, the Captains themselves were seized, taken, and carried by their own Men to the Earl; who immediately committed them to Custody, and sent them up Prisoners to the Parliament. Then the Earl communicated the Ordinance, Letters, and Votes from the two Houses, to the rest of the Officers; of whom only two more refused to continue their Charge against the signification, they had received from the King (Sir *John Mennes*, and Captain *Burly*) who were quickly difcharged and fet on fhore; and the reft, without any fcruple or hefitation, "obliged "themfelves to obey the Earl of *Warwick*, in the "Service of the Parliament;" fo that the Storm was now over, and the Parliament fully, and entirely poffeffed of the whole Royal Navy, and Militia by Sea; for they quickly difpofed of two other honeft Captains, *Kettleby*, and *Stradlin* (whom they could not corrupt) who guarded the *Irifh* Seas; and got thofe Ships likewife into their Service. And thus his Majefty was without one Ship of his own, in his three Kingdoms, at his Devotion.

As this lofs of the whole Navy was of unfpeakable ill confequence to the King's Affairs, and made his condition much the lefs confidered by his Allies, and Neighbour-Princes; who faw the Sovereignty of the Sea now in other hands, that were like to be more imperious upon the apprehenfion of any difcourtefies, than regular and lawful Monarchs ufe to be; I cannot but obferve fome unhappy circumftances, and accidents in this important bufinefs of the Navy, which looked like the hand of Providence to take that ftrength, of which his Majefty was moft confident, out of his hands. When the refolution of the Houfe of Commons, and the concurrence of the Lords was peremptory, and the Earl of *Northumberland* had declared his compliance with them, "for the fending the Earl of *Warwick* Admiral "of that Fleet, in the place of Sir *John Pennington*, "upon whom the King depended;" it was refolved likewife by them, "that Captain *Carteret*, Con- "troller of his Majefty's Navy, a Man of great "eminence, and reputation in Naval Command, "should be Vice-Admiral;" who thinking it became his near relation to his Majesty's Service, to receive his Royal pleasure before he engaged himself in any employment of that Nature, addressed himself for his directions. But the King, looking upon the Fleet in a manner taken from him, when another, whose disaffection to his Service was very notorious, was, contrary to his express pleasure, presumptuously put into the Command of it, and his own Minister displaced for no other reason (his sufficiency, and ability for command being by all Men confessed) but his Zeal and Integrity to Him, would not countenance that Fleet, and that Admiral, with suffering an Officer of his own to Command in it under the other; and therefore ordered Captain *Carteret* to decline the employment; which he, prudently and without noise, did; and thereupon, another Officer of the Navy, the Surveyor General, Captain *Battens* a Man of very different inclinations to his Master, and his Service, and furious in the new fancies of Religion, was substituted in the place: Whereas if Captain *Carteret* had been suffered to have taken that Charge, His interest and reputation in the Navy was so great, and his diligence and dexterity in Command so eminent, that it was generally believed, he would, against whatsoever the Earl of *Warwick* could have done, have preserved a Major part of the Fleet in their duty to the King. The misfortunes which happened, and are mentioned before, are not in justice to be imputed to Sir *John Pennington*; who, sure, was a very honest Gentleman, and of unshaken Faithfulness and Integrity to the King; but to the little time he had to think of it: And the perplexity he was in (besides his true Zeal to the Service) to consider that so great a work, as the recovery of the Royal Navy, was to be done by his own Personal engagement, made him look so little to his own security, that, instead of taking the Fleet from the Earl of *Warwick*, he was Himself taken by the Earl, and sent to the Parliament; where the carrying over the Lord *Digby*, and some other Jealousies, had left a great arrear of displeasure against him.

The truth is, the King was so confident upon the general Affections of the Sea-men, who were a Tribe of People more particularly countenanced and obliged by him, than other Men, his Majesty having increased their allowance, in Provision and Money, above the old establishment of the Navy, as hath been mentioned; that he did believe no Activity of ill Officers could have corrupted them; but that, when the Parliament had set out and victualled the Fleet, it would, upon any occasion, declare itself at his devotion. But, on the other side, they had been taught to believe, that all the King's bounty, and grace towards them, had flowed from the mediation of those Officers, who were now engaged against the King; and that, the Parliament having seized the Customs, and all other the Revenues of the Crown, they had no other hope of Pay or Subsistence, but by absolutely devoting themselves to their Service: so that a greater, or more general defection of any one Order of Men was never known, than that, at this time, of the Sea-men; though many Gentlemen, and some few of the Common sort, to their lasting

Honor and Reputation, either addressed themselves to the Active Service of their Sovereign, or suffered Imprisonment, and the loss of all they had, for refusing to serve against him.

The News of this diminution of his Majesty's power, and terrible addition of strength to his Enemies, was a great allay to the brisk hopes at *York*, upon the arrival of their Ammunition, and wise Men easily discerned the fatal consequence of it in opposition to the King's most hopeful designs; yet, in a very short time, all visible sense of it so much vanished, that (as there was a marvellous alacrity, at that time, in despising all advantages of the Parliament) some Men publicly, and with great confidence, averred, " that the King was a Gainer by the loss " of his Fleet; because he had no Money to pay the " Seamen, or keep them together; and that one Vic- " tory at Land, of which there was no doubt, would " restore him to his Dominion at Sea, and to what- " soever had been unjustly taken from his Majesty."

The King found it was now time to do more than write Declarations, when the Parliament was now entirely possessed of the Militia by Sea, and made such a progress in the attempt to obtain the same at Land, though the People generally (except in great Towns and Corporations, where, besides the natural Malignity, the factious Lecturers, and Emissaries from the Parliament, had poisoned their affections) and especially those of Quality, were Loyally inclined; yet, the terror of the House of Commons was so great, which sent for and grievously punished those Sheriffs and Mayors, who published, according to their Duties and express

Oaths, his Majesty's Proclamation, and those Ministers, who, according to his Injunctions, read and divulged his Declarations, that all such, and, indeed, all others eminently affected to the King, were forced to fly to *York* for Protection; or to hide themselves in Corners from that Inquisition, which was made for them. And therefore his Majesty, in the first place, that he might have one Harbour to resort to in his Kingdom, sent the Earl of *New-Castle*, privately, with a Commission to take the Government of *New-Castle*; who against the little opposition, that was prepared by the Schismatical party in the Town, by his Lordship's great Interest in those parts, the ready compliance of the best of the Gentry, and the general good Inclinations of the place, speedily and dextrously assured that most important rich Town, and Harbour to the King; which, if it had been omitted but very few days, had been seized on by the Parliament; who had then given direction to that purpose. Then for the Protection of the general parts of the Kingdom, and keeping up their affections, his Majesty appointed and sent many of the nobility and prime Gentlemen of the several Counties, who attended him, into their respective Counties to execute the Commission of Array; making the Marquis of *Hertford*, by Commission under the Great Seal of *England* (which he was to keep secret in reserve, till he found, either by the growth, or extraordinary practice of the Parliament in raising Forces, that the Commission of Array was not enough) " his Lieutenant General " of all the Western Parts of the Kingdom, with "power to Levy such a Body of Horse and Foot, "as he found necessary for his Majesty's Service, "and the containing the People within the Limits "of their Duty." With the Marquis went the Earl of *Bath* (thought then to be in notable power and interest in *Devonshire*) the Lord *Pawlet*, the Lord *Seymour*, Sir *Ralph Hopton*, Sir *John Berkley*, Sir *Hugh Pollard*, and others, very good Officers, to form an Array if it should be found expedient. And so, much of the lustre of the Court being abated by the remove of so many Persons of Honor and Quality, the King began to think of increasing, and forming his Train into a more useful posture, than it was yet; and, without any noise of raising an Army, to make the Scene of his first Action to be the recovery of *Hull*, (whither new forces were sent from *London*) by the ordinary Forces and Trained-bands of that Country; by color whereof, he hoped to have such resort, that he should need no other industry to raise such an Army, as should be sufficient to preserve himself from the violence, which threatened his safety; and accordingly, that the People might fully understand his Intentions, he summoned some of the Trained-bands to attend him at *Beverly*, a Town within four Miles of *Hull*, whither he removed his Court, and published a

The King's Proclamation from Beverly.

Proclamation, briefly containing "the Rebellion "of Sir *John Hotham*, in holding that Town by a "Garrison against him; his demanding Justice from "the two Houses without effect; the seizing his "Fleet at Sea; and the hostile Acts of Sir *John* "*Hotham* upon the Inhabitants of that Town, many

"of whom he turned out of their Habitations; and
"upon the Neigbbour-Country, by imprisoning
"many, and driving others for fear from their
"Houses: And therefore that he was resolved to
"reduce the same by Force; inhibiting all Com-
"merce or Traffic with the said Town, whilst
"it continued in Rebellion."

Which Proclamation he likewise sent to both Houses of Parliament, with this further signification, "That, before he would use force to reduce that "place to it's due Obedience, he had thought fit, "once more, to require them, that it might be "forthwith delivered to him; wherein if they should "conform themselves, his Majesty would be then "willing to admit such Addresses from them, and "return such Propositions to them, as might be "proper to settle the Peace of the Kingdom, and "compose the present Distractions. He wished them "to do their Duty, and to be assured from Him, "on the word of a King, that nothing should be "wanting on His part, that might prevent the "Calamities which threatened the Nation, and "might render his People truly happy, but if that "his gracious Invitation should be declined, God "and all good Men must judge between them:" And assigned a Day, by which he would expect their Answer at *Beverly*.

In the mean time, to encourage the good Affections of *Nottinhamshire*, which seemed almost entirely to be devoted to his Service; and to countenance and give some Life to his friends in *Lincolnshire*, where, in Contempt of his Proclamation, the Ordinance of the Militia had been boldly executed by the Lord *Willoughby of Parham*, and some Members of the House of Commons, his Majesty took a short Progress to *Newark*; and, after a day's stay, from thence to *Lincoln*; and so, by the day appointed, returned to *Beverly*; having, in both those places, been attended with such an Appearance of the Gentlemen, and Men of Quality, and so full a Concourse of the People, as one might reasonably have guessed the Affections of both those Counties would have seconded any just, and regular Service for the King.

They at *London* were not less Active; but, upon their Success in the business of the Navy, proceeded to make themselves strong enough, at least, to keep what they had; and therefore, having, by their Ordinance of the Militia, many voluntary Companies formed of Men according to their own hearts; and, by their Subscriptions, being supplied with a good stock of Money, and a good number of Horse; before the King's Message from *Beverly* came to them, on the twelfth of *July*, being the same day the Message went from the King, both Houses Voted, and Declared,

The Votes of both Houses for raising an Army.

" That an Army should be forthwith raised for the
" Safety of the King's Person; Defence of both
" Houses of Parliament, and of those, who had
" obeyed their Orders, and Commands; and preser-
" ving of the true Religion, the Laws, Liberty, and
" Peace of the Kingdom. That the Earl of *Essex*
" should be their General, and that they would Live
" and Die with him." And, having put themselves into this posture of Treating, the same day they

agreed

agreed that a Petition should be framed, "to move
"the King to a good accord with the Parliament, to
"prevent a Civil War; the which was purposely
then consented to, that the People might believe,
the talk of an Army and a General, was only to draw
the King to the more reasonable Concessions. And it
is certain, the first was consented to by many, especially of the House of Peers (in hope the better to compass the other) with the perfect horror of the thought
of a War. Though the King's Message came to them
before their own was despatched, yet, without the
least notice taken of it, and lest the contents, of their
Petition might be known before the arrival of their
own Messengers, the Earl of *Holland*, Sir *John Holland*, and Sir *Philip Stapleton*, being the Committee
appointed for the same, made a speedy and quick
Journey for *Beverly*; and arrived, in the same minute
that the King came thither from *Lincoln*: So that his
Majesty no sooner heard of the raising an Army, and
declaring a General against him, but he was encountered with the Messengers for Peace; who reported
to all whom they met, and with whom they conversed, "That they had brought so absolute a Submission from the Parliament to the King, that there
"could be no doubt of a firm and happy Peace:"
And when the Earl of *Holland* presented the Petition,
he first made a short Speech to the King; in telling
him, "That the glorious Motto of his Blessed Father,
"King *James*, was *Beati Pacifici*, which he hoped
"his Majesty would continue; that they presented
"him with the Humble Duty of his two Houses of
"Parliament, who desired nothing from him but his

BOOK V.

"consent, and acceptance of Peace; they aiming at nothing but his Majesty's Honor, and Happiness:" And then read their Message aloud, in these words:

To the King's most Excellent Majesty: The humble Petition of the Lords and Commons assembled in Parliament.

The Parliament's Petition to the King at Beverly, July 11, 1642.

"May it please your Majesty:

"Although We, your Majesty's most humble and faithful Subjects, the Lords and Commons in Parliament assembled, have been very unhappy in many former Petitions, and Supplications to your Majesty; wherein we have represented our most dutiful Affections in advising, and desiring those things, which we held most necessary for the preservation of God's true Religion; your Majesty's Safety, and Honor; and the Peace of the Kingdom: And, with much sorrow, do perceive that your Majesty, incensed by many false Calumnies and Slanders, doth continue to raise Forces against Us, and your other peaceable and Loyal Subjects; and to make great Preparations for War, both in the Kingdom, and from beyond the Seas; and by Arms and Violence, to over-rule the judgment and advice of your Great Council; and by force to determine the Questions there depending, concerning the Government and Liberty of the Kingdom: Yet, such is our earnest desire of discharging our Duty to your Majesty and the Kingdom, to preserve the Peace thereof, and to prevent the Miseries of Civil War amongst your Subjects;

"that, notwithstanding we hold ourselves bound
"to use all the means and power, which, by the
"Laws and Constitutions of this Kingdom, we are
"trusted with for Defence, and Protection thereof,
"and of the Subjects from Force and Violence: We
"do, in this our Humble and Loyal Petition, pro-
"strate ourselves at your Majesty's feet; beseeching
"your Royal Majesty, that you will be pleased to
"forbear and remove all Preparations and Actions of
"War; particularly the Forces from about *Hull*,
"from *New-Castle*, *Tinmouth*, *Lincoln*, and *Lincoln-
"shire*; and all other places. And that your Majesty
"will recal the Commissions of Array, which are
"illegal; dismiss Troops, and extraordinary Guards
"by you rais'd: That your Majesty will come
"nearer to your Parliament, and hearken to their
"faithful Advice and humble Petitions; which shall
"only tend to the defence, and advancement of Re-
"ligion; your own Royal Honor, and Safety; and
"the preservation of our Laws and Liberties. And
"we have been, and ever shall be, careful to prevent
"and punish all Tumults, and seditious Actions,
"Speeches, and Writings, which may give your
"Majesty just cause of distaste, or apprehension of
"danger. From which public Aims and Resolu-
"tions, no sinister or private respect shall ever
"make us to Decline. That your Majesty will leave
"Delinquents to the due course of Justice; and that
"nothing done, or spoken in Parliament, or by
"any Person, in pursuance of the Command and
"Direction of both Houses of Parliament, be ques-
"tioned any where but in Parliament.

"And We, for Our parts, shall be ready to lay down all those Preparations, which we have been forced to make for our defence. And for the Town of *Hull*, and the Ordinance concerning the Militia, as we have, in both these Particulars, only sought the preservation of the Peace of the Kingdom; and the defence of the Parliament from force and violence: so We shall most willingly leave the Town of *Hull* in the state it was, before Sir *John Hotham* drew any Forces into it; delivering your Majesty's Magazine into the Tower of *London*, and supplying whatsoever hath been disposed by us for the Service of the Kingdom. We shall be ready to settle the Militia by a Bill, in such a way as shall be honorable, and safe for your Majesty; most agreeable to the Duty of Parliament, and effectual for the Good of the Kingdom; that the strength thereof be not employed against itself, and that which ought to be for our Security, applied to our Destruction; and that the Parliament, and those who profess, and desire still to preserve the Protestant Religion, both in this Realm, and in *Ireland*, may not be left naked, and indefensible to the mischievous Designs, and cruel Attempts of those, who are the professed, and confederated Enemies thereof in your Majesty's Dominions, and other neighbour Nations. To which if your Majesty's Courses and Counsels shall from henceforth concur, We doubt not but We shall quickly make it appear to the world, by the most eminent effects of Love and Duty, that your Majesty's Personal Safety, your Royal Ho-

" nor, and Greatneſs, are much dearer to us than
" our own Lives and Fortunes; which We do moſt
" heartily dedicate, and ſhall moſt willingly employ
" for the ſupport, and maintenance thereof.

As ſoon as this Petition was read by the Earl of
Holland, the King told them " that the reproaches
" caſt upon him by it, were not anſwerable to the
" Expreſſions his Lordſhip had made; and that he
" was ſorry that they thought the expoſing Him,
" and his Honor to ſo much ſcandal, were the way
" to procure, or preſerve the Peace of the Kingdom:
" That they ſhould ſpeedily receive his Anſwer: by
" which the world would eaſily diſcern, Who de-
" ſired Peace moſt." And accordingly, the ſecond
day, his Majeſty delivered them, in public, his
Anſwer to their Petition, which was likewiſe read
by one of his Servants, in theſe Words:

His Majeſty's Anſwer to the Petition of the Lords
and Commons aſſembled in Parliament.

His Majeſty's Anſwer.

" Though his Majeſty had no great reaſon to be-
" lieve that the directions ſent to the Earl of *War-*
" *wick*, to go to the River *Humber*, with as many
" Ships as he ſhould think fit, for all poſſible aſſiſt-
" ance to Sir *John Hotham* (whilſt his Majeſty ex-
" pected the giving up of the Town unto him) and
" to carry away ſuch Arms from thence, as his diſ-
" cretion thought fit to ſpare out of his Majeſty's
" own Magazine: The chuſing a General by both
" Houſes of Parliament, for the defence of thoſe
" who have obeyed their Orders and Commands,
" be they never ſo extravagant, and illegal: Their

"Declaration, that, in that cafe, they would live
"and die with the Earl of *Essex* then General (all
"which were Voted the fame day with this Petition)
"And the committing the Lord Major of *London*
"to Prifon, for executing his Majefty's Writs, and
"Lawful Commands; were but ill Prologues to a
"Petition, which might compofe the miferable
"Diftractions of the Kingdom; yet his Majefty's
"paffionate defire of the Peace of the Kingdom,
"together with the Preface of the Prefenters, That
"they had brought a Petition full of duty and fub-
"miffion to his Majefty; and which defired nothing
"of him, but his confent to Peace (which his Ma-
"jefty conceived to be the Language of both Houfes
"too) begot a greedy hope, and expectation in him,
"that this Petition would have been fuch an Intro-
"duction to Peace, that it would, at leaft, have
"fatisfied his Meffage of the eleventh of this Month,
"by delivering up *Hull* unto his Majefty. But, to
"his unfpeakable grief his Majefty hath too much
"caufe to believe, that the End of fome Perfons,
"by this Petition, is not in truth to give any real
"fatisfaction to his Majefty; but, by the fpecious
"pretences of making offers to him, to miflead and
"feduce his people, and lay fome imputation upon
"him of denying what is fit to be granted; other-
"wife, it would not have thrown thofe unjuft re-
"proaches, and fcandals upon his Majefty, for ma-
"king a neceffary and juft defence for his own fafety;
"and fo peremptorily juftified fuch Actions againft
"him, as by no rule of Law or Juftice can admit
"the leaft color of defence: And, after fo many

"free and unlimited Acts of Grace passed by his
"Majesty without any condition, have proposed
"such things which, in justice, cannot be denied
"unto him, upon such conditions as, in honor,
"he cannot grant. However, that all the world
"may see how willing his Majesty would be to
"embrace any overture, that might beget a right
"understanding between Him and his two Houses
"of Parliament (with whom he is sure, he shall
"have no contention, when the private practices,
"and subtle insinuations of some few Malignant Per-
"sons shall be discovered; which his Majesty will
"take care shall be speedily done) he hath, with
"great care, weighed the Particulars of this Peti-
"tion, and returns this Answer:

"That the Petitioners were never unhappy in
"their Petitions or Supplications to his Majesty,
"while they desired any thing which was necessary,
"or convenient for the preservation of God's true
"Religion; his Majesty's Safety, and Honor; and
"the Peace of the Kingdom: And therefore, when
"those general envious Foundations are laid, his
"Majesty could wish some particular Instances had
"been applied. Let Envy and Malice object one
"particular Proposition for the preservation of God's
"true Religion which his Majesty hath refused to
"consent to; what Himself hath often made, for the
"ease of tender Consciences, and for the advance-
"ment of the Protestant Religion, is notorious by
"many of his Messages and Declarations. What
"regard hath been to his Honor and Safety, when
"he hath been driven from some of his Houses, and

"kept from other of his Towns by Force: And what care there hath been of the Peace of the Kingdom, when endeavours have been used to put all his Subjects in Arms against him, is so evident, that, his Majesty is confident, he cannot suffer by those general Imputations. It is enough that the world knows what he hath granted, and what he hath denied.

"For his Majesty's raising Forces, and making Preparations for War (whatsoever the Petitioners, by the evil Arts of the Enemies to his Majesty's Person and Government, and by the calumnies, and slanders raised against his Majesty by them, are induced to believe) all Men may know what is done that way, is but in order to his own defence. Let the Petitioners remember, that (which all the world knows) his Majesty was driven from his Palace of *White-Hall*, for safety of his Life: That both Houses of Parliament, upon their own Authority, raised a Guard to themselves (having gotten the Command of all the Trained-bands of *London* to that purpose) without the least color, or shadow of danger: That they usurped a power, by their pretended Ordinance, against all Principles and Elements of Law, over the whole Militia of the Kingdom, without, and against his Majesty's consent: That they took possession of his Town, Fort, and Magazine of *Hull*, and committed the same to Sir *John Hotham*; who shut the Gates against his Majesty, and, by Force of Arms, denied entrance thither to his own Person: That they justified this Act which they had not directed;

"and took Sir *John Hotham* into their protection for
"whatsoever he had done, or should do, against
"his Majesty. And all this, whilst his Majesty had
"no other attendance than his own Menial Servants.
"Upon this, the Duty, and Affection of this
"County, prompted his Subjects here to provide a
"small Guard for his own Person; which was no
"sooner done, but a Vote suddenly passed of his
"Majesty's intention to levy War against his Par-
"liament (which, God knows, his heart abhorreth)
"and notwithstanding all his Majesty's Professions,
"Declarations, and Protestations to the contrary,
"seconded by the clear Testimony of so great a
"Number of Peers upon the place, Propositions
"and Orders for Levies of Men, Horse, and Arms,
"were sent throughout the Kingdom; Plate and
"Money brought in, and received: Horse and Men
"raised towards an Army, Mustered, and under
"Command; and all this contrary to the Law, and
"to his Majesty's Proclamation: And a Declaration
"published, that if he should use Force for the re-
"covery of *Hull*, or suppressing the pretended
"Ordinance for the Militia, it should be held levy-
"ing War against the Parliament: And all this done,
"before his Majesty granted any Commission for
"the levying, or raising a Man. His Majesty's
"Ships were taken from him, and committed to
"the custody of the Earl of *Warwick*; who presumes,
"under that power, to usurp to himself the Sover-
"eignty of the Sea, to chase, fright, and imprison
"such of his Majesty's good Subjects, as desire to
"obey his Lawful Commands; although he had

BOOK
V.
"notice of the legal Revocation of the Earl of Nor-
"thumberland's Commission of Admiral, whereby
"all power derived from that Commission ceased.
"Let all the world now judge who begun this
"War, and upon whose account the miseries, which
"may follow, must be cast; what his Majesty could
"have done less than he hath done; and whether
"he were not compelled to make provision, both
"for the defence of himself and recovery of what is
"so violently, and injuriously taken from him; and
"whether these injuries, and indignities, are not
"just grounds for his Majesty's fears and apprehen-
"sions of further mischief, and danger to him.
"Whence the fears and jealousies of the Petitioners
"have proceeded, hath never been discovered; the
"dangers they have brought upon his Subjects are
"too evident; what those are they have prevented,
"no Man knows. And therefore his Majesty cannot
"but look upon that Charge as the boldest, and the
"most scandalous, hath been yet laid upon him;
"That this necessary provision, made for his own
"safety and defence, is to over-rule the Judgment,
"and Advice of his Great Council; and by force
"to determine the Questions there depending, con-
"cerning the Government and Liberty of the King-
"dom. If no other force had been raised to deter-
"mine those Questions, than by his Majesty, this
"unhappy misunderstanding had not been: And his
"Majesty no longer desires the blessing, and pro-
"tection of Almighty God upon Himself and his
"Posterity, than He, and They, shall solemnly
"observe the due execution of the Laws, in the

"defence of Parliaments, and the just Freedom
"thereof.

"For the Forces about *Hull*, his Majesty will
"remove them, when he hath obtained the End for
"which they were brought thither. When *Hull* shall
"be again reduced to his subjection, he will no
"longer have an Army before it. And when he
"shall be assured, that the same Necessity and pre-
"tence of Public Good, which took *Hull* from him,
"may not put a Garrison into *New-Castle* to keep the
"same against him, he will remove His from thence,
"and from *Tinmouth*; till when, the example of
"*Hull* will not out of his memory.

"For the Commissions of Array, which are legal,
"and are so proved by a Declaration now in the
"Press, his Majesty wonders why they should, at
"this time, be thought grievous, and fit to be re-
"called; if the fears of Invasion and Rebellion be so
"great, that, by an illegal pretended Ordinance,
"it is necessary to put his Subjects into a posture of
"defence, to Array, Train, and Muster them, he
"knows not why the same should not be done in a
"regular, known, lawful way. But if, in the exe-
"cution of that Commission, any thing shall be
"unlawfully imposed upon his good Subjects, his
"Majesty will take all just, and necessary care for
"their redress.

"For his Majesty's coming nearer to his Parlia-
"ment, his Majesty hath expressed himself so fully
"in his several Messages, Answers, and Declara-
"tions; and so particularly avowed a real fear of his
"safety, upon such instances as cannot be Answered,

"that he hath reason to take himself somewhat neglected, That, since upon so manifest reasons it is not safe for his Majesty to come to them, both his Houses of Parliament will not come nearer to his Majesty; or to such a place where the freedom, and dignity of Parliament might be preserved. However, his Majesty shall be very glad to hear of some such example in their punishing the Tumults (which he knows not how to expect, when they have declared, That they knew not of any Tumults; though the House of Peers desired, both for the Freedom and dignity of Parliament, that the House of Commons would join with them in a Declaration against Tumults; which they refused, that is, neglected to do) and other seditious Actions, Speeches, and Writings, as may take that apprehension of danger from him; though, when he remembers the particular complaints Himself hath made of businesses of that nature, and that, instead of inquiring out the Authors, neglect of examination hath been, when offer hath been made to both Houses to produce the Authors; as in that Treasonable Paper concerning the Militia: And when he sees every day Pamphlets published against his Crown, and against Monarchy itself; as the Observations upon his late Messages, Declarations, and Expresses; and some Declarations of their own, which give too great encouragement, in that Argument, to ill Affected Persons; his Majesty cannot, with confidence, entertain those Hopes which would be most welcome to him.

"For the leaving Delinquents to the due course of
" Justice, his Majesty is most assured there hath been
" no shelter to any such. If the tediousness and delay
" in prosecution, the vast charge in Officers fees,
" the keeping Men under a General accusation,
" without Trial, a whole year and more, and so al-
" lowing them no way for their defence and vindi-
" cation, hath frightened Men away from so charge-
" able and uncertain attendance, the Remedy is
" best provided, where the Disease grew. If the
" Law be the measure of Delinquency, none Such
" are within his Majesty's Protection: But if by De-
" linquents such are understood, who are made so
" by Vote, without any Trespass upon any known,
" or established Law: If by Delinquents those nine
" Lords are understood, who are made Delinquents
" for obeying his Majesty's Summons to come to
" him, after their stay there was neither safe, nor
" honorable, by reason of the Tumults, and other
" Violences; and whose Impeachment, he is confi-
" dent, is the greatest breach of Privilege, that,
" before this Parliament, was ever offered to the
" House of Peers: If by Delinquents such are under-
" stood, who refuse to submit to the pretended Or-
" dinance of the Militia; to that of the Navy; or to
" any other, which his Majesty hath not consented
" to; such who for the Peace of the Kingdom, in
" a humble manner, prepare Petitions to Him, or
" to both Houses, as his good Subjects of *London*
" and *Kent* did; whilst seditious ones, as that of
" *Essex*, and other places, are allowed, and Che-
" rished: If by Delinquents such are understood,

"who are called so for publishing his Proclamations,
"as the Lord Mayor of *London*; or for reading his
"Messages and Declarations, as divers Ministers
"about *London* and elsewhere; when those against
"him are dispersed with all care and industry, to
"poison and corrupt the Loyalty and Affection of
"his People: If by Delinquents such are understood,
"who have, or shall lend his Majesty Money, in
"the Universities, or in any other places: His Ma-
"jesty declares to all the world, That he will protect
"Such with his utmost power and strength; and
"directs, that, in these cases, they submit not to
"any Messengers, or Warrant; it being no less his
"Duty to Protect those who are Innocent, than to
"bring the Guilty to condign Punishment; of both
"which the Law is to be judge. And if both Houses
"do think fit to make a General, and to raise an
"Army for defence of those who obey their Orders,
"and Commands, his Majesty must not sit still,
"and suffer such who submit to his just power, and
"are solicitous for the Laws of the Land, to perish,
"and be undone, because they are called Delin-
"quents: And when They shall take upon them to
"dispense with the attendance of those who are cal-
"led by his Majesty's Writ, whilst they send them
"to Sea, to rob his Majesty of his Ships; or into
"the several Counties, to put his Subjects in Arms
"against him, his Majesty (who Only hath it) will
"not lose the power to dispense with them to attend
"his own Person; or to execute such Offices, as
"are necessary for the preservation of Himself, and
"the Kingdom; but must protect them, though they
"are called Delinquents.

"For the Manner of the proceeding against
" Delinquents, his Majesty will proceed against
" those who have no Privilege of Parliament, or
" in such cases where no Privilege is to be allowed,
" as he shall be advised by his Learned Council, and
" according to the known, and unquestionable
" Rules of the Law; it being unreasonable, that
" he should be compelled to proceed against those
" who have violated the known and undoubted
" Law, only before Them who have directed such
" violation.

" Having said thus much to the Particulars of
" the Petition, though his Majesty hath reason to
" complain, that, since the sending this Petition,
" they have beaten their Drums for Soldiers against
" him, Armed their own General with a power
" destructive to the Law, and Liberty of the Sub-
" jects; and chosen a General of their Horse: His
" Majesty, out of his Princely love, tenderness,
" and compassion of his People, and desire to pre-
" serve the Peace of the Kingdom, that the whole
" force and strength of it may be united for the
" defence of itself, and the relief of *Ireland* (in
" whose behalf he conjures both his Houses of
" Parliament, as they will answer the contrary to
" Almighty God, his Majesty, to those who trust
" them, and to that bleeding miserable Kingdom,
" that they suffer not any Moneys granted, and
" collected by Act of Parliament, to be diverted
" or employed against his Majesty; whilst his Sol-
" diers in that Kingdom are ready to mutiny, or
" perish for want of pay; and the barbarous Rebels

"prevail by that encouragement) is graciously
"pleased once more, to propose and require.
"That His Town of *Hull* be immediately delivered
"up to him: Which being done (though his Ma-
"jesty hath been provoked by unheard of Insolen-
"ces of Sir *John Hotham*'s, since his burning and
"drowning the Country, in seizing his Wine, and
"other provisions for his House, and scornfully
"using his Servant, whom he sent to require them;
"saying, it came to him by Providence, and he
"will keep it; and so refusing to deliver it, with
"threats if He, or any other of his fellow Servants,
"should again repair to *Hull* about it; and in taking
"and detaining Prisoners, divers Gentlemen, and
"others, in their passage over the *Humber* into *Lin-
"colnshire* about their necessary occasions; and
"such other indignities, as all Gentlemen must
"resent in his Majesty's behalf) his Majesty, to
"show his earnest desire of Peace, for which he
"will dispense with his own Honor, and how far
"he is from desire of Revenge, will grant a free
"and general Pardon to all Persons within that
"Town.

"That his Majesty's Magazine, taken from *Hull*,
"be forthwith put into such hands, as He shall
"appoint.

"That his Navy be forthwith delivered into such
"hands, as he hath directed for the Government
"thereof: The detaining thereof after his Majesty's
"Directions, published and received, to the con-
"trary; and employing his Ships against him in such
manner,

"manner, as they are now used, being notorious
"High-Treason in the Commanders of those Ships.
 "That all Arms, Levies, and Provisions for a
"War, made by the consent of both Houses (by
"whose Example his Majesty hath been forced to
"make some Preparations) be immediately laid
"down; and the pretended Ordinance for the Mi-
"litia and all power of imposing Laws upon the
"Subject without his Majesty's consent, be dis-
"avowed; without which, the same Pretence will
"remain to produce the same Mischief. All which
"his Majesty may as lawfully demand as to live,
"and can with no more justice be denied him, than
"his Life may be taken from him.
 "These being done, and he Parliament adjourned
"to a safe and secure place, his Majesty promises,
"in the presence of God, and binds himself by all
"his Confidence and Assurance in the Affection of
"his People, that he will instantly, and most cheer-
"fully, lay down all the Force he shall have raised,
"and discharge all his future and intended Levies;
"that there may be a general face of Peace over
"the whole Kingdom; and will repair to them:
"And desires, that all Differences may be freely
"debated in a Parliamentary way; whereby the
"Law may recover it's due reverence, the Subject
"his Just Liberty, and Parliaments themselves their
"full Vigor and Estimation; and so the whole
"Kingdom a blessed Peace, Quiet, and Prosperity.
 "If these Propositions shall be rejected, his
"Majesty doubts not of the Protection and Assist-
"ance of Almighty God, and the ready Concur-

"sence of his good Subjects; who can have no hope left them of enjoying their own long, if their King may be oppressed, and spoiled, and must be remediless. And though his Towns, his Ships, his Arms, and his Money, be gotten, and taken from him, he hath a Good Cause left, and the Hearts of his People; which, with God's blessing, he doubts not, will recover all the rest.

"Lastly, if the preservation of the Protestant Religion, the defence of the Liberty and Laws of the Kingdom, the dignity and freedom of Parliament; and the recovery, and the relief of bleeding and miserable *Ireland*, be equally precious to the Petitioners, as they are to his Majesty (who will have no quarrel but in defence of these) there will be a cheerful and speedy consent to what his Majesty hath now proposed, and desired: And of this his Majesty expects a full and positive Answer, by *Wednesday* the 27th of this instant *July*; till when, he shall not make any Attempt of force upon *Hull*, hoping in the Affection, Duty, and Loyalty of the Petitioners: And in the mean time, expects that no supply of Men be put into *Hull*; nor any of his Majesty's Goods taken from thence."

The whole Court, upon the hearing that Petition from the two Houses read, expressed a marvellous Indignation at the Intolerable Indignities offered to the King by it; and seemed no better satisfied with the Messengers; who had professed, that they brought an absolute submission to his Majesty; when in truth, what they brought, appeared to be a full Justification of whatsoever they had done before, and an implied Threat of doing worse, and fixing all the scandals upon his Majesty, which they had scattered abroad before: insomuch that all Men expected, and believed his Majesty to be engaged, for the vindication of his Princely dignity and honor, to return a much sharper Answer to them, than he had ever sent. So that, when this which is before set down (and which had before been consented to, and approved in the full Assembly of the Peers, and Counsellors) was read publicly, it was generally thought, that the King had not enough resented the Insolence, and Usurpation of the Parliament, or appeared sensible enough of the Provocations: Yet the thought of a War, which wise Men saw actually levied upon the King already, was so much abhorred, and Men were so credulous of every Expedient which was pretended for Peace, that, by the next morning (the Answer being delivered in the evening) these active Messengers for the Parliament persuaded many "that the King's " Answer was too sharp, and would provoke the " Houses, who were naturally passionate, to pro- " ceed in the high ways they were in; whereas, " if the King would abate that severity of Language, " and would yet take off the Preamble of his " Answer, they were confident, and the Earl of " *Holland* privately offered to undertake, that satis- " faction should be given to all that his Majesty " proposed." And, by this means, some were so far wrought upon, as they earnestly importuned the King, " that he would take his Answer, which "be had publicly delivered the night before, from the Messengers; and, instead thereof, return only the Matter of his own Propositions, in the most soft and gentle Language; without the Preamble, or any mention of the unjustifiable, and unreasonable demeanour of the Parliament towards him."

But his Majesty replied, "that he had for a long time, even after great provocations, and their first general Remonstrance to the People, treated with all imaginable compliance, and lenity of words with them; and discovered their unjustifiable and extravagant proceedings with and against him, and the consequences that would inevitably attend their Progress in them, with such tender expressions, as if he believed whatever was amiss to proceed from misinformation only, and unskilful mistakes: That this gentleness, and regard of his, was so far from operating upon them, that their Insolence, and Irregularities increased; and it might be from that reason, that their Messages and Declarations were writ in so high a Dialect, and with that Sovereignty of Language, as if He were subject to Their jurisdiction; and did not know but it might have some influence upon his People to his disadvantage, that is, raise terror towards Them, and lessen their reverence towards his Majesty, when all their Petitions and Propositions were more Imperative than His just, and necessary Refusals: Which condescension his Majesty had brought himself to, in hope, that His example,

"and Their natural shame, would have reformed
"that new Licence of words: That this last Address,
"under the name of a Petition (a few days after
"they had violently ravished his whole Fleet from
"him; and prepared the same day, that they had
"chosen a General, to whom they had sworn
"Allegiance, to lead an Army against him) con-
"tained a peremptory Justification of whatsoever
"they had done; and as peremptory a Threatening
"of whatsoever they could do: and therefore, if
"he should Now retract his Answer, which had
"been solemnly considered in Council, before all
"the Peers, and which in truth implied rather a
"Princely resentment of the Indignities offered to
"him, than flowed with any sharp or bitter Expres-
"sions, he should, by such yielding, give encour-
"agement to New attempts; and could not but
"much discourage those, upon whose Affections
"and Loyalty he was principally to depend; who
"could not think it safe to raise themselves to an
"indignation on his behalf, when He expressed so
"tender, or so little sense of his own sufferings:
"besides, that he was then upon an avowed Hostile
"enterprise for the reduction of *Hull*; towards
"which he was to use all possible means to draw a
"Force together, equal to that Design; and by such
"a Retraction as this proposed, and a seeming de-
"clension of his Spirit, and depending upon their
"good natures, who had done all this mischief, he
"should not only be inevitably disappointed of the
"resort of new strength, but, probably, deserted
"by those few whom he had brought together:

"That he could not reasonably, or excusably depend upon the undertaking of the Earl of *Holland*; who had so grosly deceived him in other undertakings, which were immediately in his own power to have performed: whereas neither he, nor either of the other two Gentlemen, who were joined with him in this employment, had so much interest with the Active and Prevailing Party, as to know more of their Intentions than was at present necessary to be discovered for their Concurrence.

"He said, that he had never yet consented to any one Particular, since the beginning of this Parliament, by which he had received prejudice, at the doing whereof he had not the solemn undertakings and promises of those, who were much abler to justify their undertakings, than the Earl of *Holland*; and upon whom he only depended, that it should be no disservice to him, and would be an infallible means to compass all that his Majesty desired: But he had always found those Promisers and Undertakers, though they could eminently carry on any Counsel, or Conclusion, that was against Law, Justice, or His Right, had never power to reduce, or restrain those agitations within any bounds of Sobriety, and moderation: And when they found, that many would not be guided by them, that they might seem still to Lead, themselves as furiously Followed the others; and resorted again to his Majesty with some new Expedient, as destructive as the former. So that he was resolved to rely upon God Almighty,

"and not so much to depend upon what might
"possibly prevail upon the Affections of those, from
"whom, reasonably, he could not expect any good,
"as upon such plain and avowed courses, as, let
"the success be what it would, must, to all judging
"Men, appear to be prudently, and honorably
"relied on: And therefore he positively refused to
"make the least alteration in his Answer:" And so
the Messengers departed, leaving the Court and
Country worse affected than they found it; and
branding some particular Persons, whom they found
less inclined to be ruled by their professions and
promises, "as the Authors of a Civil War:" And
making them as odious as they could, wherever
they came.

And sure, from that time, the Earl of *Holland* was
more transported from his natural temper and gentleness of disposition, into passion and animosity
against the King, and his Ministers; and, having been
nothing pleased with his own condition at *London*,
finding the Earl of *Essex* (whom he did not secretly
love, and did indeed contemn) to draw all Men's
Eyes towards him, and to have the greatest Interest
in their hearts, he had seriously intended, under
color of this Message to the King, to discover if
there were any sparks yet left in his Royal breast,
which might be kindled into affection, or acceptation of his Service; and hoped, if he could get any
credit, to redeem his former trespasses: But when
he not only found his Majesty cold towards him,
but easily enough discerned, by his reception, that
all former inclinations were dead, and more than

BOOK V.

ordinary prejudices grown up towards him in their places, and that his advices were rejected, he returned with rancor equal to the most furious he went to; and heartily joined and concurred towards the suppressing that Power, in the Administration whereof he was not like to bear any part.

His Majesty having, by his Answer, obliged himself not to make any forcible Attempt upon *Hull* till the 27th of *July*, by which time he might reasonably expect an Answer to his Propositions, in the mean time resolved to make some short progress into the neighbour Counties; and accordingly, the same day the Messengers departed, the King went to *Doncaster*; and the next day to *Nottingham*; and so to *Leicester*; where he heard, the Earl of *Stamford*, and some other Parliament-Men, were executing the Ordinance of the Militia: But, before his Majesty came thither, they removed themselves to *Northampton*; a Town so true to them, as, if they had been pursued, would have shut their Gates against the King Himself, as *Hull* had done.

At *Leicester* the King was received, with great expressions of Duty and Loyalty, by the appearance of the Trained-bands, and full Acclamations of the People; yet there were two Accidents that Happened there, which, if they be at all remembered, will manifest, that if the King were Loved there as he ought to be, that the Parliament was more Feared than He. It happened to be at the time of the general Assizes, and Justice *Reeve* (a Man of a good reputation for Learning, and Integrity; and who, in good times, would have been a good Judge) sat

there as Judge; and Mr. *Henry Haſtings*, younger Son to the Earl of *Huntingdon*, was purpoſely made high Sheriff, to contain the County within the limits of their duty by the power of that Office, as well as by the Intereſt, and Relation of his Family. The Earl of *Stamford*, and his Aſſiſtants, had departed the Town but few hours before his Majeſty's entrance; and had left their Magazine, which was indeed the Magazine of the County, in a little Store-Houſe at the end of the Town, guarded by ſome inferior Officers whom they had brought down to Train and Exerciſe the Militia, and other Zealous and devoted Men of the County, in all to about the Number of 25, who had barricadoed the door of the Houſe; and profeſſed " to keep it againſt all demanders; having proviſions within it of all ſorts. The King was very unwilling (coming in ſo peaceable a manner, at ſo peaceable a time) to take any notice of it. On the other hand, it was an Act of too great inſolence to be ſuffered; and, upon the matter, to leave a Garriſon of the Rebels in poſſeſſion of the Town; and therefore he ſent word to the Judge, " that if He took not ſome legal way to
" remove ſuch a Force ſo near his Majeſty, his Ma-
" jeſty would do it in ſome Extraordinary courſe:" Which, upon the ſudden, would have puzzled him to have done; having neither Soldier, Cannon, nor Powder to effect it; the want of which as much troubled the Sheriff. In the end, the Gentlemen of the Country, who had not yet otherwiſe declared themſelves on either ſide, than by waiting on his Majeſty, finding that the King would not go from

the Town, till that Nuisance was removed; and that it might bring Inconveniences, Charge, and Mischief to the County of a high nature; so prevailed, that, as his Majesty was contented to take no notice of it, so they within the House, in the night, upon assurance of Safety, and Liberty to go whither they would, removed and left the House; and so that matter was quieted.

The other Accident was, or was like to have proved, more Ridiculous: Some of the King's Servants, hearing that the Earl of *Stamford*, and the other Militia-Men were newly gone out of the Town, had of Themselves, coming thither before the King, galloped after them; intending to have apprehended them, and brought them before the King; and, though the other were too fleet for them, had, in the way, overtaken Dr. *Bastwick*, a Man well known, who had been a principal Officer with them at *Leicester*, and fled at the same time, but could not keep pace with his Commanders: Him they brought to the Town, where, by the Sheriff, he was committed to Prison; having confessed enough Treason, and justifying it, as would have justly hanged any Subject. The King thought once to have had him indicted then, at the Assizes, upon the plain Statute of 25 *E.* III. But the Judge besought his Majesty not to put a matter of so great moment, upon which the power of the two Houses of Parliament, and a Parliament sitting, must be determined, before one single Judge, whose reputation was not enough to bear so great a burden; however, he declared his own opinion fully to his Ma-

jesty, "that it was Treason; which, he believed, all
"the other Judges must acknowledge; and if con-
"vened together by his Majesty to that purpose,
"he thought a joint Declaration, and Resolution
"of all together might be of great use to the King;
"whereas the publishing of His particular opinion
"could only destroy himself, and nothing advance
"his Majesty's Service: Besides, he had no reason
"to be so confident of the Country, as to conclude
"that a Jury, then suddenly summoned, would
"have courage to find the Bill; and then their Not
"doing it, if it 'were attempted, would prove a
"greater countenance to the Ordinance, than the
"Votes of the two Houses had yet given it." This
last reason gave his Majesty satisfaction; so that he
was contented that the fellow should be kept in
Prison, and the Trial be deferred, till he could conveniently summon more Judges to be present.

His Majesty was no sooner persuaded to be content that this prosecution might be suspended, but
the close Agents for the Parliament's Service, who
were not yet discovered but appeared very entire
to the King, so dextrously carried themselves, that
they prevailed with those Gentlemen of the Country,
whose Zeal to his Majesty was most eminent and
unquestionable, and even with the Judge himself,
"to wish, that his Majesty would freely and gra-
"ciously discharge the Dr. of his Imprisonment;" or
give the Judge leave to do so upon a *Habeas Corpus*
(which he was advised to require) "And that it
"would be such an Act of Mercy, and singular
"Justice, that would not only work upon the People

"of That County to his Majesty's advantage, but
"must have a great influence upon the whole Kingdom, and even upon the Parliament itself." And with this strange desire the good Judge, and those principal Gentlemen, confidently came to the King, the night before he intended to return Northward. His Majesty told them, "he would think of it till the next morning." And, in the mean time, concluding by what he heard, that though he should refuse to discharge him, or to consent that he should be discharged, his restraint would not be long in that place after His departure, the People already resorting to him with great Licence, and the Dr. according to his Nature, talking seditiously and loudly, he directed "a Messenger of the Chamber "very early, with such Assistance as the Sheriff "should give him, to carry him away to *Notting-* "*ham;* and by the help of that Sheriff, to the Goal "at *York:*" Which was executed accordingly with expedition, and secrecy; if either of which had been absent, it is certain the Common People had rescued him; which, of how trivial a moment soever it shall be thought, I could not but mention as an Instance of the Spirit and Temper of that time, and the great Disadvantage the King was upon, that so many very good Men thought fit, at a time, when very many hundreds of Persons of Honor, and Quality, were imprisoned with all strictness and severity by the Parliament, upon the bare suspicion that they meant to go to the King, or that they wished well to him, or for not submitting to some illegal Order, or Command of Theirs, that the King should

OF THE REBELLION.

discharge an infamous Person, taken in an Act of High Treason, and who more frankly and avowedly professed sedition, than he did the Science of which he pretended to be Doctor.

The King, according to his appointment, returned towards *Hull*, in expectation of an Answer from the Parliament; which came two days after the appointed day, but with no solemnity of Messengers, or other ceremony than inclosed to one of the Secretary's to be presented to the King; in which they told him,

The Parliament's Replication, July 26. 1642.

"That they could not, for the present, with the discharge of the Trust reposed in them for the safety of the King and Kingdom, yield to those Demands of his Majesty: the reason why they took into their custody the Town of *Hull*, the Magazine, and Navy; passed the Ordinance of the Militia; and made preparations of Arms; was for security of Religion, the safety of his Majesty's Person, of the Kingdom, and Parliament; all which they did see in evident, and imminent danger; from which when they should be secured, and that the Forces of the Kingdom should not be used to the destruction thereof, they should then be ready to withdraw the Garrison out of *Hull*; to deliver the Magazine and Navy; and settle the Militia, by Bill, in such a way as should be honorable and safe for his Majesty; most agreeable to the duty of Parliament; and effectual for the good of the Kingdom; as they had professed in their late Petition. And for Adjourning the Parliament, they apprehended no reason for his

BOOK V.
"Majesty to require it; nor security for themselves to consent to it. And as for that reason which his Majesty was pleased to express, they doubted not but the Usual place would be as safe for his Royal Person, as any other; considering the full Assurance they had of the Loyalty, and Fidelity of the City of *London* to his Majesty; and the care which his Parliament would ever have to prevent any danger, which his Majesty might justly apprehend; besides the manifold conveniences to be had there, beyond any other parts of the Kingdom. And as for the laying down of Arms; when the causes which moved them to provide for the defence of his Majesty, the Kingdom, and Parliament, should be taken away, they should very willingly, and cheerfully forbear any further Preparations, and lay down their Force already raised."

Which Replication, as they called it, to his Majesty Answer, they ordered "to be Printed, and read in all Churches, and Chapels within the Kingdom of *England*, and Dominion of *Wales*.

And so the War was now denounced, by their express Words against his Majesty; as it had been long before in their Actions; and both Parties seemed to give over all thoughts of further Treaties, and Overtures; and each prepared to make themselves considerable by the strength, and power of such Forces, as they could draw together.

In *London* they intended nothing but the forming of their Army, and such other things of power, as were in order thereunto. To that purpose, the Bill for the payment of Tonnage and Poundage being expired, on the first day of *July*, and they having sent another of the same nature to the King for his consent, for six Months longer, his Majesty, since he saw That, and all other Money properly belonging to him, violently taken from him, and employed by them against him, refused to give his Royal Assent thereunto: Whereupon, without the least hesitation (albeit it had been enacted this very Parliament, "that whosoever should presume to pay, or "receive that duty, after the expiration of the Act, "before the same was granted to his Majesty with "the consent of the Lords and Commons, should "be in a Præmunire;" which is the heaviest punishment inflicted by Law, but the Loss of Life) they appointed and ordered by the Power of the two Houses (which they called an Ordinance of Parliament) "that the same duty should be continued; "and declared that they would save all Persons con- "cerned, from any Penalty or Punishment what- "soever:" By, which they now became possessed of the Customs, in their own right.

Towards such, as any ways (though under the obligation of Oaths or Offices) opposed, or discountenanced what they went about, they proceeded with the most extravagant severity that had been ever heard of; of which I shall only mention two Instances; the First, of the Lord Mayor of *London*, Sir *Richard Gurney*, a Citizen of great Wealth, Reputation, and Integrity; whom the Lords had, upon the complaint of the House of Commons, before their sending the last Petition to the King (of which his Majesty gave them a touch in his Answer) committed to the Tower of *London*: for causing the King's Proclamation against the Militia, by virtue of his Majesty's Writ to him directed, and according to the known Duty of his place, to be publicly proclaimed. And shortly after, that they might have a Man more compliant with their designs to govern the City, notwithstanding that he insisted upon his innocence, and made it appear that he was obliged by the Laws of the Land, the Customs of the City, and the Constitution of his Office, and his Oath, to do whatsoever he had done: He was by their Lordships, in the presence of the Commons, adjudged " to be put out of his Office of Lord Mayor of *Lon-* " *don;* to be utterly incapable of bearing Office in " City or Kingdom, and of all Honor or Dignity; " and to be imprisoned, during the pleasure of the " two Houses of Parliament." And, upon this sentence, Alderman *Pennington,* so often before mentioned, was, by the noise and clamor of the Common People, against the Customs and Rules of Election, made Mayor; and accordingly installed; and the true, old, worthy Mayor committed to the Tower of *London;* where, with notable constancy, he continued almost to his Death.

The other Instance, I think fit to mention, is that of Judge *Mallet;* who, as is before remembered, was committed to the Tower the last Lent, for having seen a Petition prepared by the grand Jury of *Kent*, for the Countenance of the Book of Common-Prayer, and against the imposition of the Militia by Ordinance without the Royal Assent. This Judge (being, this Summer-Circuit, again Judge of Assize for those

Counties)

Counties) sitting at *Maidstone* upon the great Assize, some Members of the House of Commons, under the Style and Title of a Committee of Parliament, came to the Bench; and, producing some Votes, and Orders, and Declarations of one or both Houses, " required him, in the name of the Parliament, to " cause those Papers (being on the behalf of the Or- dinance of the Militia, and against the Commission of Array) " to be read." He told them, " that he sat " there by virtue of his Majesty's Commissions; and " that he was authorized to do any thing comprised " in those Commissions; but he had no Authority " to do any thing else; and therefore, there being " no mention, in either of his Commissions, of those " Papers, or the Publishing any thing of that nature, " he could not, nor would not do it;" and so (finding less respect and submission, than they expected, both to their Persons and their Business, from the Learned Judge, and that the whole County, at least the prime Gentlemen and the Grand Jury, which represented the County, contemned both much more) this Com- mittee returned to the House with great exclamations against Mr. Justice *Mallet*, " as the Fomenter and " Protector of a Malignant Faction against the Par- " liament. And, upon this Charge, a Troop of Horse was sent to attend an Officer; who came with a Warrant from the Houses, or some Committee (whereas Justice *Mallet*, being an Assistant of the House of Peers, could not Regularly be summoned by any other Authority) to *Kingston* in *Surry*, where the Judge was keeping the general Assizes for that County; and, to the unspeakable Dishonor of the

Public Justice of the Kingdom, and the Scandal of all Ministers or Lovers of Justice, in that violent manner took the Judge from the Bench, and carried him Prisoner to *Westminster*; from whence, by the two Houses, he was committed to the Tower of *London*; where he remained for the space of above two years, without ever being charged with any particular Crime, till he was redeemed by his Majesty by the exchange of another, whose liberty they desired.

By these heightened Acts of Power and Terror, they quickly demonstrated, how unsecure it would be for any Man, at least not to concur with them. And, having a General, Arms, Money, and Men enough at their devotion, they easily formed an Army, publicly disposing such Troops and Regiments, as had been raised for *Ireland*, and, at one time, one hundred thousand pounds of that Money, which, by Act of Parliament, had been paid for that purpose, towards the constituting that Army, which was to be led against their Lawful Sovereign. So that it was very evident, they would be in such an Equipage within few Weeks, both with a Train of Artillery, Horse and Foot, all taken, armed, furnished, and supplied out of his Majesty's own Magazines and Stores, that they had not reason to fear any opposition. In the mean time, they declared, and published to the People, "that they raised that Army, "only for the defence of the Parliament, the King's "Person, and the Religion, Liberty, and Laws of "the Kingdom, and of those, who, for Their "sakes, and for those Ends, had obeyed their Orders:

"That the King, by the inſtigation of evil Coun-
"ſellors, had raiſed a great Army of Papiſts; by
"which he intended to awe, and deſtroy the Parlia-
"ment; to introduce Popery, and Tyranny: Of
"which intention, they ſaid, his requiring *Hull*:
"his ſending out Commiſſions of Array; beſpeaking
"Arms and Ammunition beyond the Seas (there
"having been ſome brought to him by the Ship
"called the Providence) his declaring Sir *John Ho-*
"*tham* Traytor; and the putting out the Earl of
"*Northumberland* from being Lord High-Admiral
"of *England*; his removing the Earls of *Pembroke*,
"*Eſſex*, *Holland*, the Lord *Fielding*, and Sir *Henry*
"*Vane*, from their ſeveral places and employments;
"were ſufficient and ample evidences: And there-
"fore, they conjured all Men, to aſſiſt their Ge-
"neral, the Earl of *Eſſex*." And, for their better
and more ſecret tranſaction of all ſuch Counſels, as
were neceſſary to be entered upon, or followed,
they made a Committee, of ſome choice Members
of either Houſe, to intend the great buſineſs of the
Kingdom with reference to the Army; who had Authority, without ſo much as communicating the
matter to the Houſe, to impriſon Perſons, ſeize upon
their Eſtates; and many other Particulars, which
the two Houſes, in full Parliament, had not the leaſt
Regular, Legal, Juſtifiable Authority to do. And
for the better encouragement of Men to engage in the
Service, the Lord *Kimbolton*, and the five Members
of the Houſe of Commons, formerly accuſed by his
Majeſty of High-Treaſon, upon ſolemn debate, had
ſeveral Regiments conferred on them; and, by their

example, many other Members of both Houses, some upon their lowness, and decayedness of their Fortunes, others to get name and reputation to be in the number of Reformers (amongst whom they doubted not all Places of Honor, or Offices of profit, would be bestowed) most upon the confidence, that all would be ended without a Blow, by the King's want of power to gather strength, desired and obtained Command of Horse or Foot; their Quality making amends for their want of experience, and their other defects; which were repaired by many good Officers both English, and Scots; the late Troubles having brought many of that tribe to *London*, and the reputation of the Earl of *Essex* having drawn others, out of the Low-Countries, to engage in that Service. In the choice of which Officers, whilst they accused the King of a purpose to bring a Foreign Force, and of entertaining Papists, they neither considered Nation nor Religion; but entertained all Strangers, and Foreigners, of what Religion soever, who desired to run their Fortune in the War.

On the other side, Preparations were not made with equal expedition, and success by the King, towards a War: For, though he well understood, and discerned, that he had nothing else to trust to, he was to encounter strange Difficulties to do that. He was so far from having Money to levy, or pay Soldiers, that he was, at this very time, compelled for very real want, to let fall all the Tables kept by his Officers of State in Court, by which so many of all qualities subsisted; and the Prince, and Duke of

York, eat with his Majesty; which Table only was kept. And whoever knows the Constitution of a Court, well knows what indispositions naturally flow from those declensions; and how ill those Tempers bear any diminution of their own Interests; and being once indisposed themselves, how easily they infect others. And that which made the present want of Money the more intolerable, there was no visible hope from whence supply could come, in any reasonable time: And that which was a greater want than Money, which Men rather feared than found, there were no Arms; for, notwithstanding the fame of the great Store of Ammunition, brought in by that Ship, it consisted only in truth of Cannon, Powder, and Bullet, with eight hundred Musquets, which was all the King's Magazine. So that the hastening of Levies, which at that time was believed would not prove difficult, would be to little purpose, when they should continue unarmed. But that which troubled the King more than all these real incapacities of making War, was the temper and constitution of his own Party; which was compounded, for the most part, in Court, Council, and Country, of Men drawn to him by the impulsion of Conscience, and abhorring the unjust and irregular proceedings of the Parliament; otherwise unexperienced in Action, and unacquainted with the Mysteries, and necessary Policy of Government; severe observers of the Law, and as scrupulous in all matters relating to it, as the other pretended to be. All his Majesty's Ancient Counsellors, and Servants (except some few of lasting Honor, whom We shall have occasion often to mention) that they might redeem former oversights, or for other unworthy designs, being either publicly against him in *London*, or privately discrediting his Interest and Actions, in his own Court. These Men still urged "the execution of the Law; that what extravagances soever the Parliament practised, the King's observation of the Law would, in the end, suppress them all." And, indeed, believed the raising a War to be so wicked a thing, that they thought it impossible the Parliament should intend it, even when they knew what they were doing. However they concluded, "that he that was forwardest in the preparing an Army, would be first odious to the People; by the affections of whom, the other would be easily suppress."

This was the general received Doctrine; and though it appeared plainly to others (of equal affection to the Public Peace) how fatal those Conclusions, in that sense in which they were urged, must prove to the whole Kingdom; and how soon the King must be irrecoverably lost, if he proceeded not more vigorously in his defence; yet even those Men durst not, in any formed and public Debate, declare themselves; or speak that plain English the State of Affairs required; but satisfied themselves with speaking, what they thought necessary, to the King in Private; by which means the King wanted those firm, and solid foundations of Counsel and Foresight, that were most necessary for his condition: So that he could neither impart the true motives, and grounds of any important Action, nor discover the utmost of his Designs. And so he still seemed (notwithstanding the greatest, and avowed preparations of the Enemy) to intend nothing of Hostility, but in order to the reducing of *Hull;* the benefit of which he hoped, would engage the Trained-bands of that great County (which was the sole strength he yet drew thither) till he could bring other Forces thither, which might be fit for that, or any other Design.

But there was another Reason of his Majesty's going to, and staying at *Beverly*, than was understood; and, it may be, if it had been known, might have produced a better Effect; which I think necessary to insert in this place. The Lord *Digby*, whom We have mentioned before, in the first disorder, by which the King and Queen were driven from *London*, to have left *England*, and to be after unreasonably accused by the House of Commons of High-Treason, had remained from that time in *Holland;* and, hearing the King's condition at *York*, to be so much improved beyond what he left it at *Windsor*, had, with some Commands from the Queen, arrived there very privately, and stayed some days in a disguise at *York*, revealing himself to very few Friends, and speaking with the King in so secret a manner in the night, that no notice was taken of his being there; and, finding the King's Affairs not in so good a posture as he expected, and conceiving it yet not fit for him to appear, resolved to return again to the Queen, and to hasten that provision of Arms and Ammunition, without which it was not possible for the King to resist any violence that threatened him; and so, in the same Bark which brought him over, he went again to Sea for *Holland*, with *Wilmot*, *Ashburnham*,

BOOK V.

Pollard, and *Berkeley*; who purposely removed themselves from Court, upon the clamor of the Parliament, till the King was ready to use their Service. They were not many hours at Sea, when they met the Providence (which We mentioned before) with the Ammunition, which was only wanted; and, well knowing her, they agreed, "that *Wilmot*, *Pollard*, " and *Berkeley*, should return with the Ammuni- " tion to the King; and *Digby*, and Col. *Ashburn- " ham*, should pursue their former Intentions for " *Holland*." But their Parties continued so long, that the Parliament-Ships, who had watched and chased the Providence, came up to them; and though the Ship escaped, and run on shore, as was before mentioned, yet the Fly-boat, in which the Lord *Digby* was, could not so well get away; but was taken by them, and carried in with so much the more triumph into *Hull*, that they had been disappointed of their greater Prize. Col. *Ashburnham*, though he was in great umbrage with the Parliament, and one of those Delinquents, whom they reproached the King with, was so well known to Sir *John Hotham*, with whom he stood in a good degree of familiarity, that he could not dissemble or conceal himself; but the Lord *Digby*, being in so real a disguise that his nearest friends would not easily have known him, pretended to be a Frenchman, whose Language he spoke excellently; and seemed to be so Sea-sick, that he kept himself in the hole of the Bark, till they came to *Hull*; and, in that time, disposed of such Papers as were not fit to be perused; and when he came on Shore, so well contertened sickness, and want of health, that he easily procured himself to be sent, under a Guard, to some obscure corner for repose; whilst Col. *Ashburnham*, who was the only Prisoner they thought worth the looking after, was carefully carried to the Governor; who received him with as much Civility, as he could reasonably expect.

The Lord *Digby*, being by himself, quickly considered the desperateness of his condition: "That it would not be possible to conceal himself long, being so well known to many who were in the *Providence*, and the Garrison quickly knowing whatsoever was spoken of in the Country: That he was, how unjustly, or unreasonably soever, the most odious Man in the Kingdom to the Parliament; into whose hands if he should then come, his Life would be, at least, in apparent hazard:" And how to get himself out of that Labyrinth was very difficult, since Sir *John Hotham* was so far from any inclination of kindness towards him, as he had owned to Col. *Ashburnham*, that he was in the Number of his most notorious Enemies. However, in this eminent extremity (as he is a Man of the greatest presence of mind, and the least appalled upon danger, that I have known) he resolved, not to give himself over; and found means to make one of his Guard, in broken English, which might well have become any Frenchman, understand, "that he desired to speak privately with the Governor; and that he would discover some Secrets of the King's, and Queen's to him, that would highly advance the Service of the Parliament." The Fellow made haste

to let the Governor know these good tidings; who understanding French well, as speedily sent for the Frenchman; who was brought before him in the presence of much company, and without any disorder, gave such an account of himself, as they understood him to have seen much of the French Service (of which he spoke very fluently) and to have come over recommended to the King for some Command, if he should have occasion to use Soldiers; as, he said, People abroad conceived him likely to have. After he had entertained the company with such discourse, there being present some Gentlemen, who came lately out of *France*, and so being the more curious to administer questions, he applied himself to the Governor; and told him, "that if he might be ad-
" mitted to privacy with him, he would discover
" somewhat to him, which he would not repent to
" have known." The Governor, who was a Man apt enough to fear his own safety, but more apprehensive of the Jealousies which would attend him (for his eldest Son, and some others, were more absolutely confided in by the Parliament than himself, and were in truth, but Spies over him) would not venture himself in another Room; but drew him to a great Window at a convenient distance from the company, and wished him " to say what he thought
" fit." The Lord *Digby*, finding he could not obtain more privacy, asked him, in English, " whe-
" ther he knew him? the other, surprised, told him,
" *No;* Then, said he, I shall try whether I know
" Sir *John Hotham*; and whether he be, in truth,
" the same Man of Honor, I have always taken him

"to be:" And, thereupon, told him who he was; and "that he hoped he was too much a Gentleman to deliver him up a sacrifice to their rage and fury, who, he well knew, were his implacable Enemies." The other, being astonished, and fearing that the By-standers would discover him too (for, being now told who he was, he wondered he found it not out Himself) he desired him "to say no more for the present; that he should not be sorry for the trust he reposed in him, and should find him the same Man he had thought him: That he would find some time, as soon as conveniently he might, to have more conference with him. In the mean time, that he should content himself with the ill accommodation he had: the amendment whereof would beget suspicion: and so he called the Guard, instantly to carry him away, and to have a very strict Eye upon him;" and turning to the Company, and being conscious to himself of the trouble and disorder in his Countenance, told them, "that the Frenchman was a shrewd Fellow, and understood more of the Queen's Counsels and designs, than a Man would suspect: That he had told him that which the Parliament would be glad to know; to whom presently he would make a despatch, though he had not yet so clear informations, as, he presumed, he should have after two or three days:" And so departed to his Chamber.

It was a wonderful influence, that this Noble Person's Stars (which used to lead him into, and out of the greatest perplexities and dangers, throughout the whole course of his Life) had upon this whole affair. *Hotham* was, by his nature and education, a rough and a rude Man; of great covetousness, of great pride, and great ambition; without any Bowels of good nature, or the least sense, or touch of generosity; his parts were not quick and sharp, but composed, and he judged well; he was a Man of craft, and more like to deceive, than to be cozened: Yet, after all this, this young Nobleman, known, and abhorred by him, for his admirable faculty of Dissimulation, had so far prevailed, and imposed upon his spirit, that he resolved to Practice that Virtue, which the other had imputed to him; and not to suffer him to fall into the hands of his Enemies. He sent for him, the next day, at an hour when he was more vacant from attendants, and observers; and, at first, told him his resolution; " that, since he had so frankly put himself into his " hands, he would not deceive his Trust;" and wished him " to consider, in what way, and by " what color, he should so set him at Liberty, that " he might, without any other danger, arrive at " the place where he would be. For, he said, he would " not trust any Person living with the Secret, and " least of all his Son;" whom he mentioned with all the bitterness imaginable, " as a Man of an ill nature, " and furiously addicted to the worst designs the " Parliament had, or could have; and One that " was more depended upon by them than Himself, " and sent thither only as a Spy upon him." From hence he entered upon the discourse " of the times, " and mischief that was like to befal the whole King- " dom, from the difference between the King and

" the Parliament." Then lamented his own Fate, that, being a Man of very different Principles from those who drove things to this extremity, and of entire affection and duty to the King, he should now be looked upon as the Chief ground, and cause of the Civil War which was to ensue, by his not opening the Ports, when the King would have entered into the Town:" Of which business, and of all the circumstances attending it, he spake at large; and avowed, " that the information sent him of the King's purpose presently to hang him, was the true cause of his having proceeded in that manner."

The Lord *Digby*, who knew well enough how to cultivate every period of such a discourse, and how to work upon those Passions which were most predominant in him, joined with him in the sense of the Calamities, which were like to befal the Nation; which he bewailed Pathetically; and, " that it should be in the power of a handful of ill Men, corrupted in their Affections to the King, and against Monarchy itself, to be able to involve him, and many others of his clear intentions, in their dark Counsels, and to engage them to prosecute ends which they abhorred, and which must determine in the ruin of all the undertakers. For, he told him, that the King, in a short time, would reduce all his Enemies: That the hearts of the People were already, in all places, aliened from them; and that the Fleet was so much at the King's disposal, that, as soon as they should receive his Orders, they would appear in any

"place he appointed: That all the Princes in *Christen-*
"*dom* were concerned in the quarrel, and would
"engage in it, as soon as they should be invited to
"it: And that the Prince of *Orange* was resolved to
"come over in the head of his Army, and would
"take *Hull* in three days." All which ought, reasonably, to have been true in the Practice, though it had very little ground in the Speculation. And when he had, by degrees, amused and terrified him with this discourse, he enlarged upon "the Honor and
"Glory, that Man would have, who could be so
"blessed, as to prevent this terrible Confusion, that
"was in view: That King and People would join
"in rewarding him with Honors, and Preferments
"of all kind; and that his Name would be derived
"to Posterity, as the Preserver of his Country He
"told him, He was that Man, that could do all
"this; that, by delivering up *Hull* to the King, he
"might extinguish the War; and that immediately
"a Peace would be established throughout the
"Kingdom: That the world believed, that he had
"some credit both with the King; and Queen; that
"he would employ it all in his Service; and if he
"would give him this rise to begin upon, he should
"find, that he would be much more solicitous for
"His greatness, and a full recompence for his merit,
"than he was now for his own safety." All these Advertisements, and reflections, were the subject of more than one discourse; for Sir *John Hotham* could not bear the variety, and burden of all those thoughts together; but within two days all things were adjusted between them. *Hotham* said,

" it would not become him, after such a refusal,
" to put the Town into the King's hands; nor could
" he undertake (if he resolved) to effect it; the
" Town itself being in no degree affected to his
" Majesty's Service; and the Trained-bands, of
" which the Garrison wholly consisted, were under
" Officers upon whom he could not depend. But,
" he said, if the King would come before the Town,
" though but with one Regiment, and plant his
" Cannon against it, and make but one shot, he
" should think he had discharged his Trust to the
" Parliament, as far as he ought to do; and that he
" would immediately then deliver up the Town;
" which he made no doubt but that he should be then
" able do do." And, on this errand, he was contented the Lord *Digby* should go to the King, and be conducted out of the Town beyond the limits of danger; the Governor having told those Officers he trusted most, that " he would send the Frenchman
" to *York*; who, he was well assured, would return
" to him again." He gave him likewise a note to a Widow, who lived in that City, at whose House he might lodge, and by whose hands he might transmit any Letters to him.

When he came to *York*, and after he had spoke with the King, it was resolved, he should appear in his own likeness, and wait upon the King in public, that it might be believed, that he had Transported himself from *Holland* in the Ship that brought the Ammunition; which was hardly yet come to *York*, it being now about the time that Mr. *Villiers*, and Sir *John Pennington* had been sent away, and before the

BOOK V.

news came of their ill success. This was the cause of the sudden March towards *Hull*, before there was a Soldier levied to make an Assault, or maintain a Siege; which was so much wondered at then, and so much censured afterwards. For as soon as his Majesty received this assurance, which he had so much reason to depend upon by the treatment the Lord *Digby* had received, he declared, " he would, " upon such a day, go to *Beverly*," a place within four miles of *Hull*; and appointed three or four Regiments of the Country, under the Command of such Gentlemen whose affection was unquestionable, to march thither, as a Guard to his Person: and likewise sent a little Train of Artillery, which might be ready for the Summons. When his Majesty was ready with this Equipage for his March the Lord *Digby* returned again in his old disguise to *Hull*, to make sure that all things there might correspond with the former obligation. As soon as the King, and the whole Court (for none remained at *York*) came to *Beverly* (where they were all accommodated, which kept them from being quickly weary) and the Trained-bands were likewise come thither, the General, the Earl of *Lindsey*, first took possession of his Office; a little troubled, and out of countenance, that he should appear the General without an Army; and be engaged in an Enterprise, which he could not imagine would succeed. His Majesty ordered him to send out some Officers, of which there was a good store, to take a view of the Town, and of such advantage-ground, within distance, upon which he might raise a Battery; as if he meant on a sudden to assault the place;

Whereupon the King goes to Beverly with design upon Hull, but in vain.

OF THE REBELLION.

place; which appeared no unreasonable design; if there were a good Party in the Town to depend upon. And yet the General had no opinion, that his Army of Trained-bands would frankly expose themselves to such an Attack: Besides a great number of Officers, and Persons of Quality, who were all well Horsed, and had many Servants as well provided, the King had his Troop of Guards so continued, as hath been said before; and there were few Horse in *Hull*, and those without Officers who understood that kind of Service. So that it was no hard matter to take a very full view of the Town, by riding to the very Ports, and about the Walls; nor, at first appearance, was there any show of Hostility from the Town upon their nearest approaches to it; but after they had made that visit two or three days together, they observed that the Walls were better manned, and that there was every day an increase of laborers repairing the Works; and then they begun to Shoot, when any went within distance of the Works.

All this while Sir *John Hotham* had tried some of his Officers, in whose particular affection he had most confidence, how far they were like to be governed by him; and found them of a temper not to be relied upon. His Son was grown jealous of some design, and was caballing with those who were most notorious for their disaffection to the Government; and new Officers were sent down, by the Parliament, to assist in the defence of the Town, which, they thought, might probably be attempted; and supplies of Men had been taken in from the Ships, and had been sent thither from *Boston*, a Town, upon the

BOOK V.

same Coast, of eminent disloyalty. So that, when the Lord *Digby* returned thither, he found a great damp upon the spirit of the Governor, and a sadness of mind, that he had proceeded so far; of which his Lordship made all the haste he could to advertise the King; but his Letters must first be sent to *York* before they could come to *Beverly*; and, when they were received, they contained still somewhat of hope, " that he should be able to restore him to his " former courage, and confirm his resolution:" So that the King seemed to defer any attempt, upon the hopes of the Earl of *Holland's* Message before mentioned, and, in the end, he was compelled to give over the design, all hope from the Governor growing desperate; whether from his want of Courage, or want of Power to execute what he desired, remains still uncertain. When Sir *John Hotham* gave over further thoughts of it, he dismissed both the Lord *Digby*, and Col. *Ashburnham*, whom he had likewise detained till then, as a Man of use in the execution of the design, with many professions of Duty to the King. and as the concealing those two Persons, and afterwards releasing them, immediately increased the jealousy of the Parliament against him, so it was the Principal cause, afterwards, of the loss of his Head.

The King dismissed the Trained-bands, and returned with his Court to *York*, in so much less credit than when he came from thence, as the entering into a War without power, or preparation to prosecute it, was like to produce. The inconvenience was the greater, because the principal Persons of Quality,

OF THE REBELLION.

of Court or Country, and the Officers, had the less reverence for the King's conduct, by seeing such an Action entered upon with so little reason, and prosecuted so perfunctorily: All which reproaches his Majesty thought fitter to bear, than to discover the Motives of his Journey; which were then known to few, nor, to this day, have been published.

When the King returned to *York*, exceedingly troubled at the late March he had made, and all Men expressing great impatience to be in Action, very many Persons of Honor and Quality, having attended long at Court, believing they might be more useful to his Majesty's Service in their own Countries, in restraining the disaffected from any seditious attempts, and disposing the People in general to be constant in their Loyalty, an Accident fell out, that made it absolutely necessary for the King to declare the War, and to enter upon it, before he was in any degree ripe for Action; which was, that *Portsmouth* had declared for the King, and refused to submit to the Parliament; which had thereupon sent an Army, under the Command of Sir *William Waller*, to reduce it. The relating how this came to pass, requires a large discourse, and will administer much variety, not without somewhat of pleasure and wonder, from the temper and spirit of the Person who conducted that Action; if it can be said to be conducted without any Conduct.

We have remembered before, in the last year, the discourse of the bringing up the Army to *London* to awe the Parliament, and the unspeakable dishonor, and damage the King sustained by that discourse,

BOOK V.

Col Goring, at Portsmouth, declares for the King.

BOOK V.

how groundless soever it was; all which was imputed to Col. *Goring*, who, by that means, grew into great reputation with the Parliament, as a Man so irrecoverably lost at Court, that he would join with them in the most desperate designs; yet he carried himself with so great dexterity, that, within few Months, he wrought upon the King and Queen to believe, that he so much repented that fault, that he would redeem it by any Service; and to trust him to that degree, that the Queen, once, resolved, when the tumults drove their Majesties first from *London*, for her security, to put herself into *Portsmouth*, which was under his Government, whilst his Majesty betook himself to the Northern parts: which design was no sooner over (if not before) than he, again, intimated so much of it to the Lord *Kimbolton*, and that Party, that they took all the trust he had from Court, to proceed from the confidence their Majesties had of his Father's interest in him; whose Affection, and Zeal to their Service was ever most indubitable: but assured themselves; He was their own, even against his own Father. So that he carried the matter so, that, at the same time, he received 3000l. from the Queen (which she raised by the sale of her Plate, and some Jewels) to fortify, and victual, and reinforce his Garrison, against the time it should be necessary to declare for the King; and a good supply from the Parliament, for the payment of the Garrison, that it might be kept the better devoted to Them, and to Their Service. All which he performed with that admirable dissimulation, and rare confidence, that, when the

House of Commons was informed by a Member, whose Zeal, and Affection to them was as much valued as any Man's, "that all his correspondence in the County was with the most Malignant Persons; that of those, many frequently reforted to, and continued with him in the Garrison; that he was fortifying, and raising of Batteries towards the Land: And that, in his discourse, especially in the seasons of his good fellowship, he used to utter threats against the Parliament," and sharp censures of their Proceedings, and upon such Informations (the Author whereof was well known to them, and of great reputation; and lived so near *Portsmouth*, that he could not be mistaken, in the matter of fact) the House sent for him, most thinking he would refuse to come; Colonel *Goring* came, upon the Summons, with that undauntedness, that all clouds of distrust immediately vanished, insomuch as no Man presumed to whisper the least jealousy of him; which he observing, came to the House of Commons, of which he was a Member; and, having sat a day or two patiently, as if he expected some Charge, in the end he stood up, with a countenance full of modesty, and yet not without a mixture of anger (as he could help himself with all the insinuations of doubt, or fear, or shame, or simplicity in his face, that might gain belief, to a greater degree than I ever saw any Man; and could seem the most confounded when he was best prepared, and the most out of countenance when he was best resolved, and to want words, and the habit of speaking, when they flowed from no Man with greater power) and told them, "that he had "been sent for by them, upon some information "given against him, and that, though he believed, "the Charge being so ridiculous, they might have "received, by their own particular inquiry, satis- "faction; yet the discourses that had been used, "and his being sent for in that manner, had begot "some Prejudice to him in his Reputation; which "if he could not preserve, he should be less able to "do Them service; and therefore desired, that he "might have leave (though very unskilful, and "unfit to speak, in so wise and judicious an Assem- "bly) to present to them the state and condition "of that Place under his Command; and then he "doubted not but to give them full satisfaction in "those Particulars, which, possibly, had made "some impression in them to his disadvantage: "That he was far from taking it ill from those, who "had given any information against him; for, what "he had done, and must do, might give some "Umbrage to well affected Persons, who knew not "the grounds and reasons, that induced him so to "do; but that if any such Person would, at any "time, resort to him, he would clearly inform "them of whatever Motives he had; and would "be glad of their Advice, and Assistance for the "better doing thereof." Then he took notice of every particular that had been publicly said against him, or privately whispered, and gave such plau- sible Answers to the whole, intermingling sharp taunts, and scorns, to what had been said of him, with pretty application of himself, and flattery to

the Men that spake it: Concluding, "that they well
" knew, in what esteem he stood with others: so
" that if, by his ill carriage, he should forfeit the
" good opinion of that House, upon which he
" only depended, and to whose Service he entirely
" devoted himself, he were mader than his Friends
" took him to be, and must be as unpitied in any
" misery, that could befal him, as his Enemies
" would be glad to see him." With which, as innocently and unaffectedly uttered, as can be imagined,
he got so general an Applause from the whole House,
that, not without some little Apology for troubling him, "they desired him again to repair to his
" Government, and to finish those Works, which
" were necessary for the safety of the place;" and
gratified him with consenting to all the Propositions,
he made in behalf of his Garrison, and paid him a
good Sum of Money for their Arrears; with which,
and being privately assured (which was indeed resolved on) that he should be Lieutenant General
of their Horse in their new Army, when it should
be formed, he departed again to *Portsmouth*; in the
mean time, assuring his Majesty by those who were
trusted between them, "that he would be speedily
" in a Posture to make any such Declaration for his
" Service, as she should be required;" which he was
forced to do sooner than he was provided for it,
though not sooner than he had reason to expect.

When the Levies for the Parliament Army were
in good forwardness, and that Lord had received
his Commission for Lieutenant General of the Horse,
he wrote to the Lord *Kimbolton*, who was his most

bosom Friend, and a Man very powerful, desiring, "that he might not be called to give his attendance "upon the Army, till it was ready to march; be- "cause there were so many things to be done, and "perfected, for the safety of that important Place, "that he was desirous to be present Himself at the "work as long as was possible. In the mean time, "he had given directions to his Agent in *London*, "to prepare all things for his equipage; so that he "would be ready to appear, at any Rendezvous, "upon a day's warning." Though the Earl of *Essex* did much desire his company, and assistance in the Council of War, and preparing the Articles, and forming the Discipline for the Army, he having been more lately versed in the Order and Rule of Marches, and the provisions necessary, or convenient thereunto, than any Man then in their Service, and of greater Command than any Man but the General; yet the Lord *Kimbolton* prevailed, that he might not be sent for, till things were riper for Action. And, when that Lord did afterwards write to him, "that it was time he should come away," he sent such new, and reasonable excuses, that they were not unsatisfied with his delay; till he had multiplied those excuses so long, that they begun to suspect; and they no sooner inclined to suspicion but they met with abundant Arguments to cherish it. His behaviour and course of Life was very notorious to all the Neighbours, nor was he at all reserved in his mirth, and public Discourses, to conceal his opinion of the Parliament, and their Proceedings. So that, at last, the Lord *Kimbolton* writ plainly to him, "that he could no longer excuse his absence "from the Army, where he was much wanted; "and that, if he did not come to *London* by such a "short day, as he named, he found his Integrity "would be doubted; and that many things were "laid to his charge, of which he doubted not his "innocence; and therefore conjured him, imme- "diately, to be at *Westminster*; it being now to be "no longer deferred, or put off." He writ a jolly Letter to that Lord, "that, the truth was, his "Council advised him, that the Parliament did "many things which were illegal; and that he might "incur much danger by obeying all their Orders; "that he had received the Command of that Garri- "son from the King; and that he durst not be absent "from it, without His leave:" And concluded with some good Counsel to the Lord.

This Declaration of the Governor of a place, which had the reputation of being the only place of strength in *England*, and situated upon the Sea, put them into many apprehensions; and they lost no time in endeavouring to reduce it; but, upon the first understanding his resolution, Sir *William Waler* was sent, with a good part of the Army, so to block it up, that neither Men, nor Provision, might be able to get in; and some Ships were sent from the Fleet, to prevent any relief by Sea: And these advertisements came to the King, as soon as he returned to *York*.

It gave no small reputation to his Majesty's Affairs, when there was so great a damp upon the spirits of Men, from the misadventures at *Beverly*, that so notable a place as *Portsmouth* had declared for him, in the very beginning of the War; and that so good an Officer as *Goring*, was returned to his duty, and in the possession of the Town: And the King, who was not surprised with the matter, knowing well the resolution of the Colonel, made no doubt, but that he was very well supplied with all things, as he might well have been, to have given the Rebels work for three, or four Months, at the least. Whereupon, he forthwith published a Declaration, that had been long ready, in which he recapitulated all the Insolent, and Rebellious Actions the two Houses had committed against him; and declared them "to " be guilty; and forbid all his Subjects to yield any " obedience to them:" And, at the same time, published his Proclamation; by which, he " required " all Men, who could bear Arms, to repair to him " at *Nottingham*, by the 25th of *August* following; " on which day, he would set up his Royal Standard " there, which all good Subjects were obliged to " attend." At the same time, he sent the Marquis of *Hertford* to raise Forces in the West, or, at least to restrain those parts (where His Interest, and Reputation was greater than any Man's) within the limits of their Duty to the King, and from being corrupted, or perverted by the Parliament; and with him went the Lord *Seymour*, his Brother; the Lords *Pawlet*, *Hopton*, *Stawel*, *Coventry*, *Berkely*, *Windham*, and some other Gentlemen, of the prime Quality, and Interest in the Western parts; who were like to give as good examples in their Persons, and to be followed by as many Men, as any such

Number of Gentlemen in *England* could be. And, from this Party, enlivened by the power, and reputation of the Marquis, the King was in hopes, that *Portsmouth* would be shortly relieved, and made the head-quarter to a good Army. When all this was done, he did all that was possible to be done, without Money, to hasten his Levies of Horse and Foot, and to prepare a light train of Artillery; that he might appear at *Nottingham*, at the day when the Standard was to be set up, with such a body of Men, as might be, at the least, a competent Guard to his Person.

Many were then of opinion, " that it had been
" more for his Majesty's benefit and Service, if the
" Standard had been appointed to be set up at *York*;
" and so that the King had stayed there, without
" moving further South, until he could have marched
" in the head of an Army, and not to depend upon
" gathering an Army up in his March. All the Nor-
" thern Counties were, at present, most at his de-
" votion; and so it would be most easy to raise Men
" there: *New-Castle* was the only Port in his obe-
" dience, and whither he had appointed his supplies
" of Arms, and Ammunition to be sent; of which
" he had so present need, that all his Magazine,
" which was brought in the Providence, was already
" distributed to those few Gentlemen, who had re-
" ceived Commissions, and were most like speedily
" to raise their Regiments; and it would be a very
" long, and might prove a very dangerous passage
" to get the supplies, which were daily expected,
" to be brought with security from *New-Castle*, when

"the King should be advanced so many days Journey "beyond *York*." All which were very important considerations, and ought to have prevailed; but the King's inclinations to be nearer *London*, and the expectation he had of great effects from *Portsmouth*, and the West, disposed him to a willingness to prefer *Nottingham*; but that which determined the Point, was an apparent, and manifest aversion in the *Yorkshire* Gentlemen, whose affections were least suspected, that his Majesty should continue, and remain at *York*; which, they said, the People apprehended, "would inevitably make that Country the seat of the "War:" unskilfully imagining, that the War would be no where, but where the King's Army was; and therefore they facilitated all things, which might contribute to his remove from thence; undertook, to provide Convoys for any Arms and Ammunition from *New-Castle*; to hasten the Levies in their own Country; and to borrow the Arms of some of the Trained-bands; which was the best expedient, that could be found out, to arm the King's Troops, and had it's reverse in the murmurs it produced, and in leaving the best affected Men, by being disarmed, at the Mercy of their Enemies; who carefully kept their Weapons, that they might be ready to fight against the King. This caused the resolution to be taken for *Nottingham*, without enough weighing the objections, which, upon the Entrance into great Actions, cannot be too much deliberated, though, in the Execution, they were best shut out. And it quickly appeared in those very Men, who prevailed most in that Council; for, when the time drew on,

in which his Majesty was to depart, and leave the Country. Then they remembered, "that the Gar-
"rison of *Hull* would be left as a thorn in their
"sides, where there were well formed, and active
"Troops, which might march over the Country
"without control, and come into *York* itself without
"resistance: That there were many disaffected Per-
"sons of Quality, and Interest in the Country, who,
"as soon as the King should be gone, would appear
"amongst their neighbours, and find a concurrence
"from them in their worst designs; and that there
"were some places, some whole Corporations, so
"notoriously disaffected, especially in matters relat-
"ing to the Church, that they wanted only Con-
"ductors to carry them into Rebellion."

These, and the like reflections, made too late impressions upon them; and Now, too much, they magnified this Man's power, whom before they contemned; and doubted that Man's Affection, of which they were before secure; and made a thousand Propositions to the King this day, whereof they rejected the greatest part to morrow; and, as the day approached nearer for the King's departure, their apprehensions and irresolutions increased. In the end, they were united in two Requests to the King; that "he would commit the supreme Command of
"the Country, with reference to all Military Affairs,
"to the Earl of *Cumberland*; and qualify him, with
"an ample Commission, to that purpose." The other, "that his Majesty would command Sir *Tho-*
"*mas Glemham* to remain with them, to govern
"and command such Forces, as the Earl of *Cumber-*

"*land* should find necessary for their defence." And this Provision being made by the King, they obliged themselves to concur in making any preparations, and forming any Forces the Earl should require. His Majesty, as willingly, gratified them in both their desires. The Earl of *Cumberland* was a Man of great Honor and Integrity, who had all his Estate in that Country, and had lived most amongst them, with very much acceptation, and affection from the Gentlemen, and the Common People: but he was not, in any degree, active, or of a Martial temper; and rather a Man more like not to have any Enemies, than to oblige any to be firmly, and resolutely his Friends, or to pursue his Interest: The great Fortune of the Family was divided, and the greater part of it carried away by an Heir Female; and his Father had so wasted the remainder, that the Earl could not live with that lustre, nor draw so great a dependance upon him, as his Ancestors had done. In a word, he was a Man of Honor, and Popular enough in Peace, but not endued with those parts which were necessary for Such a season. Sir *Thomas Glemham* was a Gentleman of a noble extraction, and a fair Fortune, though he had much impaired it; he had spent many years, in Armies, beyond the Seas; and he had been an Officer of very good esteem in the King's Armies, and of courage, and Integrity unquestionable; but he was not of so stirring and active a nature, as to be able to infuse Fire enough into the Flegmatic constitutions of that People, who did rather wish to be Spectators of the War, than Parties in it; and believed, if they did not provoke the other Party, they might all live quietly together; until Sir *John Hotham*, by his excursions, and depredations out of *Hull*, and their seditious Neighbours, by their Insurrections, awakened them out of that Pleasant Dream. And then the greatest part of the Gentry of that Populous Country, and very many of the Common People, did behave themselves with signal Fidelity, and Courage in the King's Service: Of all which Particulars, which deserve well to be remembered, and transmitted to Posterity, there will be occasion to make mention, in the following Discourse.

Yet I cannot leave *York* without the mention of one Particular; which, in truth, is a lively Instance of the Spirit and Temper of that time, and was a sad Presage of all the misfortunes which followed. There were very few Gentlemen, or Men of any Quality, in that large County, who were actively or factiously disaffected to his Majesty; and of those the Lord *Fairfax*, and his Son, Sir *Thomas Fairfax*, were the chief; who were governed by two or three, of inferior Quality, more conversant with the People; who were as well known as They. All these were in the County, at their Houses, within few miles of *York*; and the King resolved, at his going away, to have taken them all Prisoners, and to have put them in safe Custody; by which, it was very probable, those mischiefs, that shortly after broke out, might have been prevented. But the Gentlemen of the County, who were met together to consult for their own security, hearing of this Design, besought his Majesty "Not to do it;" alledging, "that he would, "thereby, leave them in a worse condition, by an Act so ungracious, and unpopular; and that the disaffected would be so far from being weakened, that their Party would be increased thereby;" many really believing, that neither Father nor Son were transported with over-vehement inclinations to the Parliament; but would willingly sit still, without being Active on either side; which, no doubt, was a Policy, that many, of those, who wished well, desired and intended to be safe by. And so his Majesty left *York*, taking with him only two or three of inferior rank (whereof one *Stapleton* was one) who were known to have been very active in stirring the People to Sedition; and yet, upon some specious pretences, some very good Men were persuaded, within few days, to procure the Liberty and Enlargement even of those from his Majesty. So ticklish were those times, and so wary were all Men to advise, the King should do any thing, which, upon the strictest inquisition, might seem to swerve from the strict rule of the Law; believing, unreasonably, that the softest and gentlest Remedies might be most wholesomely applied to those rough, and violent Diseases.

The King came to *Nottingham* two or three days before the day he had appointed to set up the Standard; having taken *Lincoln* in his way, and drawn some Arms from the Trained-bands of that County with him to *Nottingham*; from whence, the next day, he went to take a view of his Horse; whereof there were several Troops well armed, and under good Officers, to the number of seven or eight hundred Men;

Men; with which, being informed, "that there were some Regiments of Foot marching towards Coventry, by the Earl of *Essex* his Orders, he made haste thither;" making little doubt, but that he should be able to get thither before them, and so to possess himself of that City; and he did get thither the day before they came; but found, not only the Gates shut against him, but some of his Servants shot, and wounded from the Walls: Nor could all his Messages, and Summons prevail with the Mayor and Magistrates, before there was any Garrison there, to suffer the King to enter into the City. So great an Interest, and Reputation the Parliament had gotten over the Affections of that People, whose hearts were alienated from any reverence to the Government.

The King could not remedy the Affront, but went that night to *Stonely*, the House then of Sir *Thomas Lee*; where he was well received; and, the next day, his Body of Horse, having a clear view, upon an open Campaign, for five or six miles together, of the Enemies small Body of Foot, which consisted not of above twelve hundred Men with one Troop of Horse, which Marched with them over that plain, retired before them, without giving them one Charge; which was imputed to the ill conduct of *Wilmot*, who Commanded; and had a colder Courage, than many who were under him, and who were of opinion, that they might have easily defeated that Body of Foot: Which would have been a very seasonable Victory; would have put *Coventry* unquestionably into the King's hands, and sent him with a good Omen to the setting up of his Standard. Whereas, that unhappy Retreat, which looked like a Defeat, and the Rebellious behaviour of *Coventry*, made his Majesty's return to *Nottingham* very Melancholy; whither he returned the very day the Standard was appointed to be set up.

The King's Standard set up at Nottingham Aug. 15, 1642.

According to the Proclamation, upon the twenty-fifth day of *August*, the Standard was erected, about six of the Clock in the evening of a very stormy, and tempestuous day. The King himself, with a small train, rode to the top of the *Castle-Hill*, *Varney* the Knight-Marshal, who was Standard-Bearer, carrying the Standard, which was then erected, in that place, with little other Ceremony than the sound of Drums, and Trumpets: Melancholy Men observed many ill Presages about that time. There was not one Regiment of Foot yet brought thither, so that the Trained-bands, which the Sheriff had drawn together, were all the strength the King had for his Person, and the Guard of the Standard. There appeared no Conflux of Men in obedience to the Proclamation; the Arms, and Ammunition were not yet com- from *York*, and a General Sadness covered the whole Town. The Standard was blown down, the same night it had been set up, by a very strong and unruly wind, and could not be fixed again in a day or two, till the tempest was allayed. This was the Melancholy State of the King's Affairs, when the Standard was set up.

END OF THE FOURTH VOLUME.

www.ingramcontent.com/pod-product-compliance
Lightning Source LLC
Chambersburg PA
CBHW021347230426
43666CB00006B/436